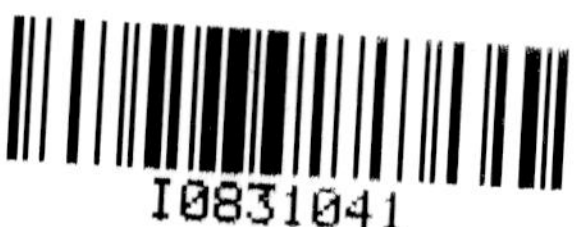

This Coloring Book

Belongs To

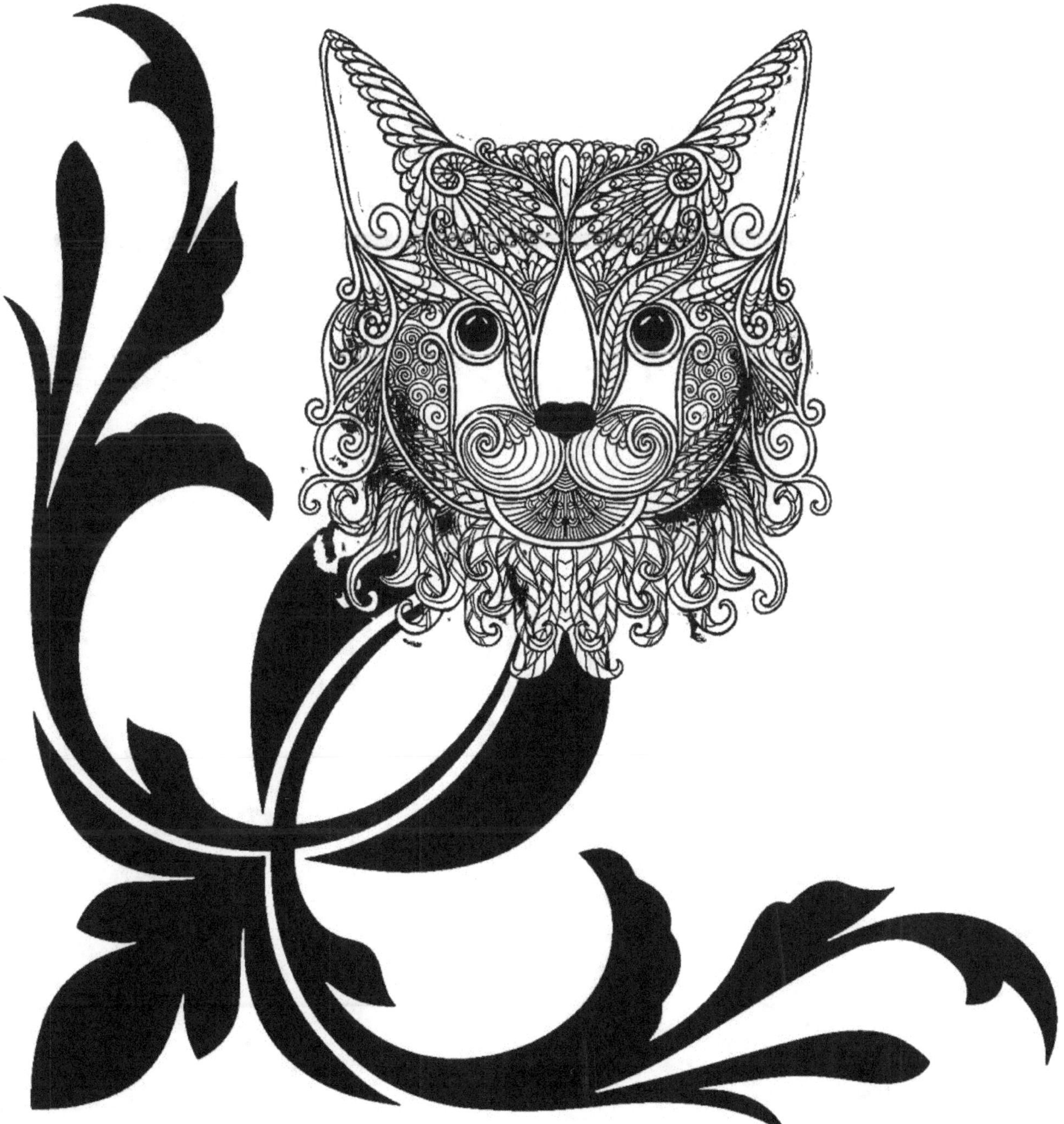

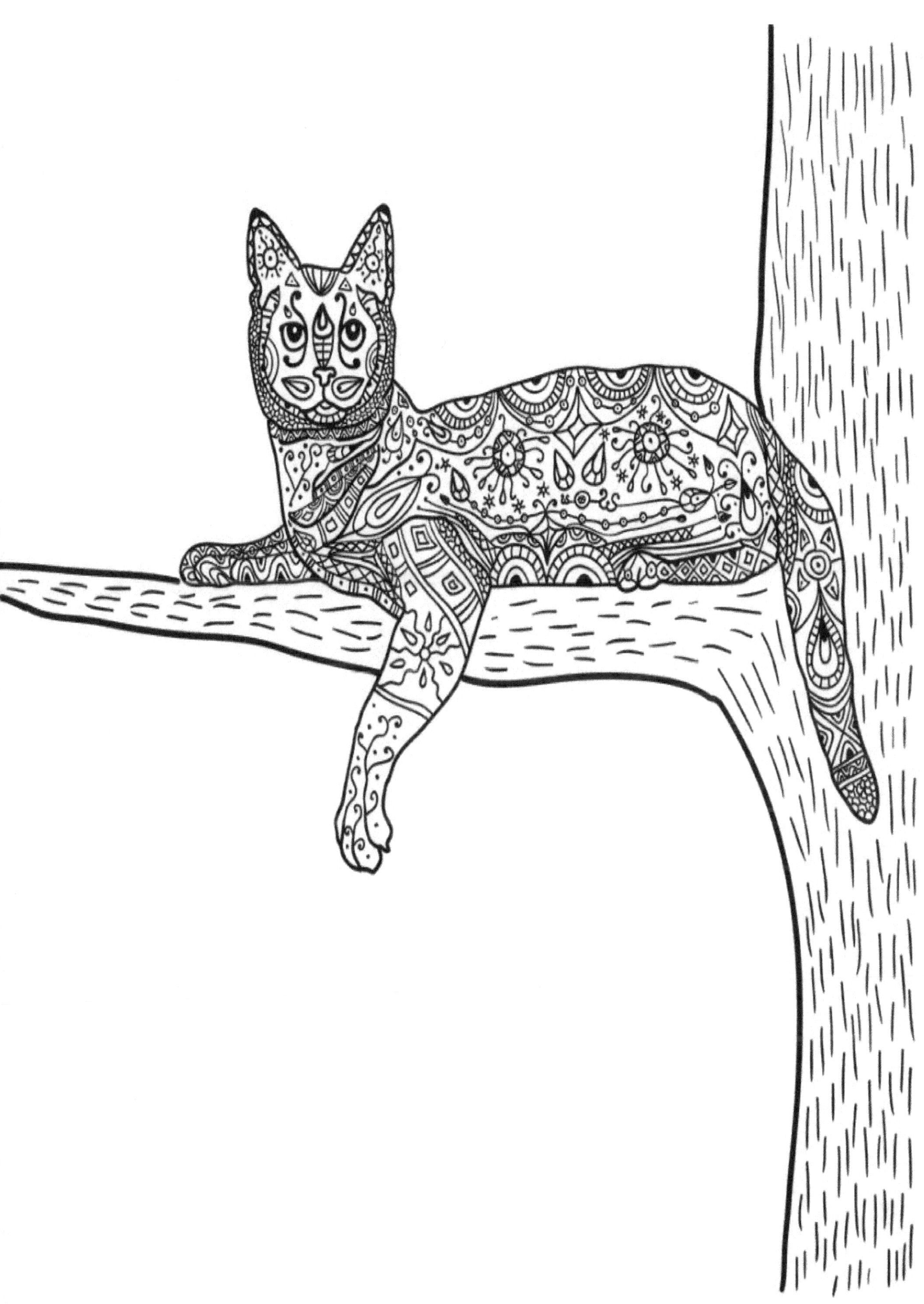

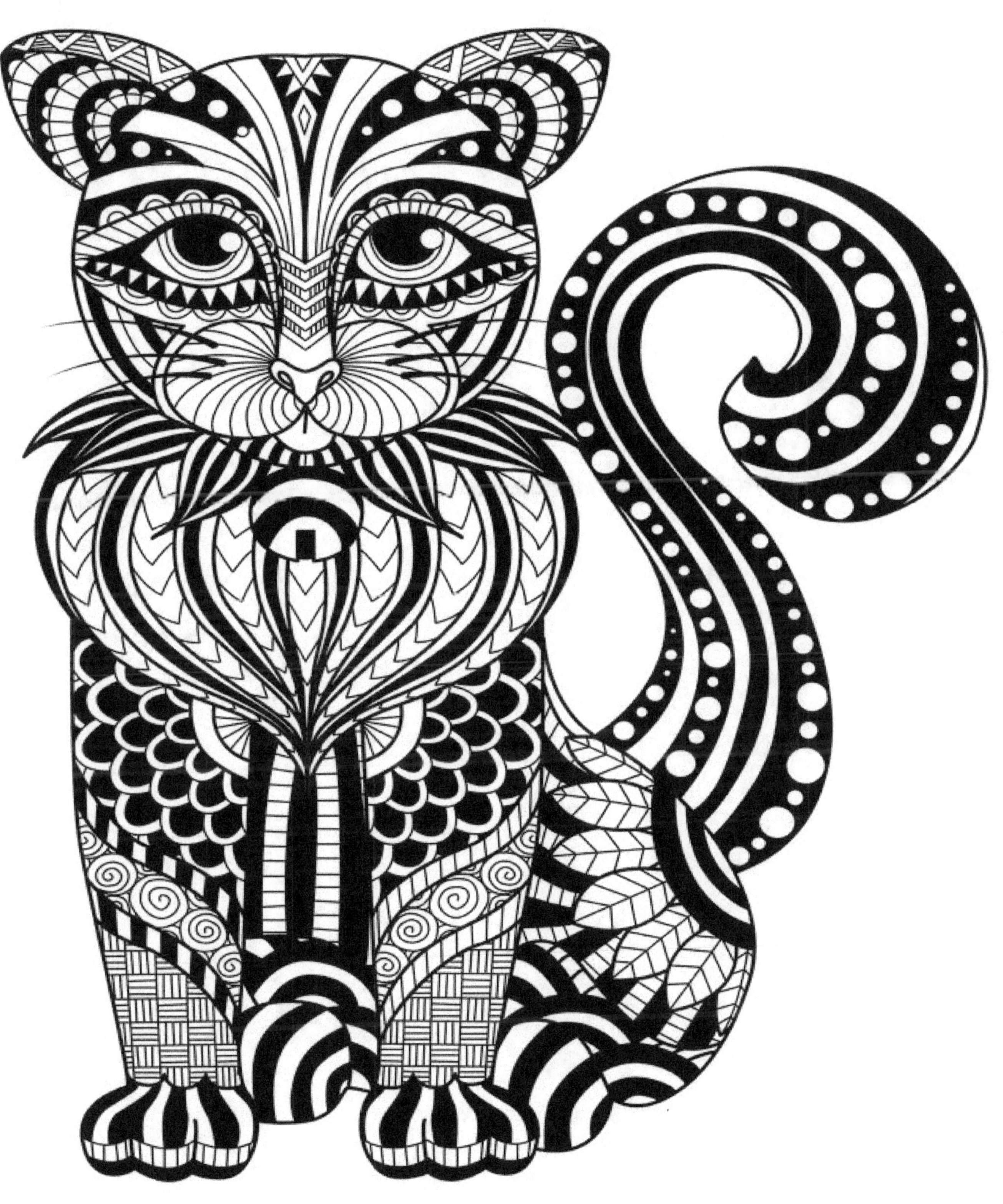

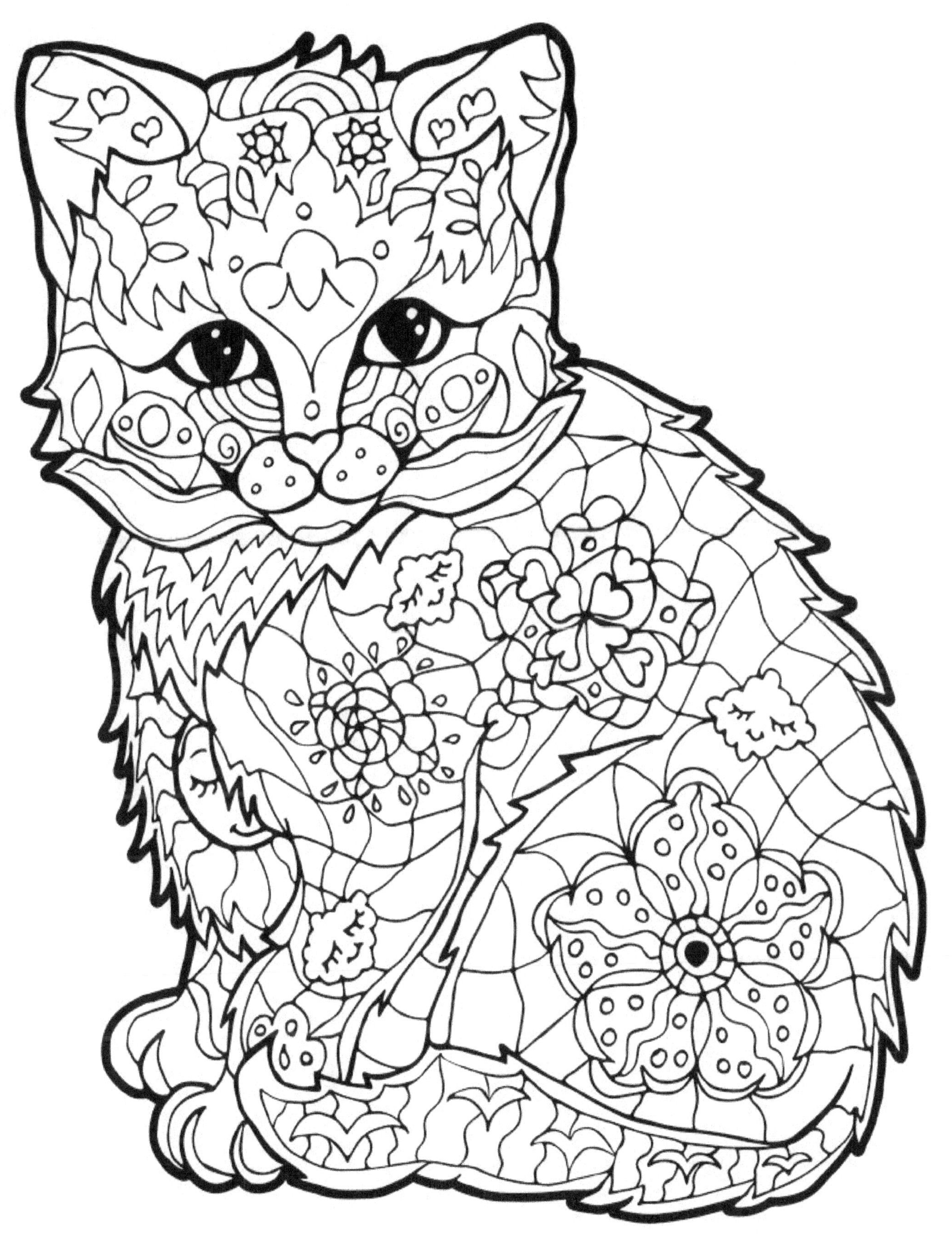

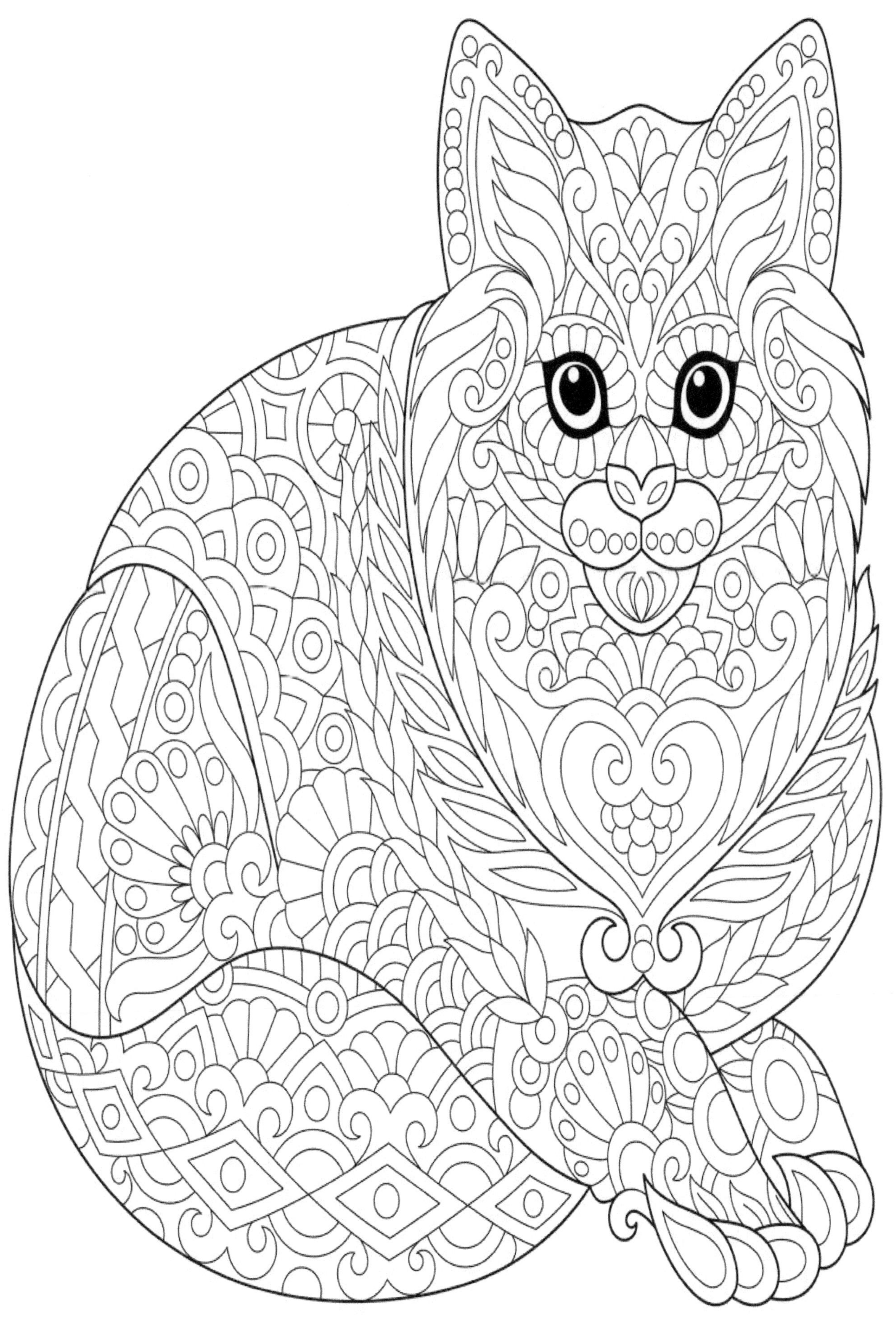

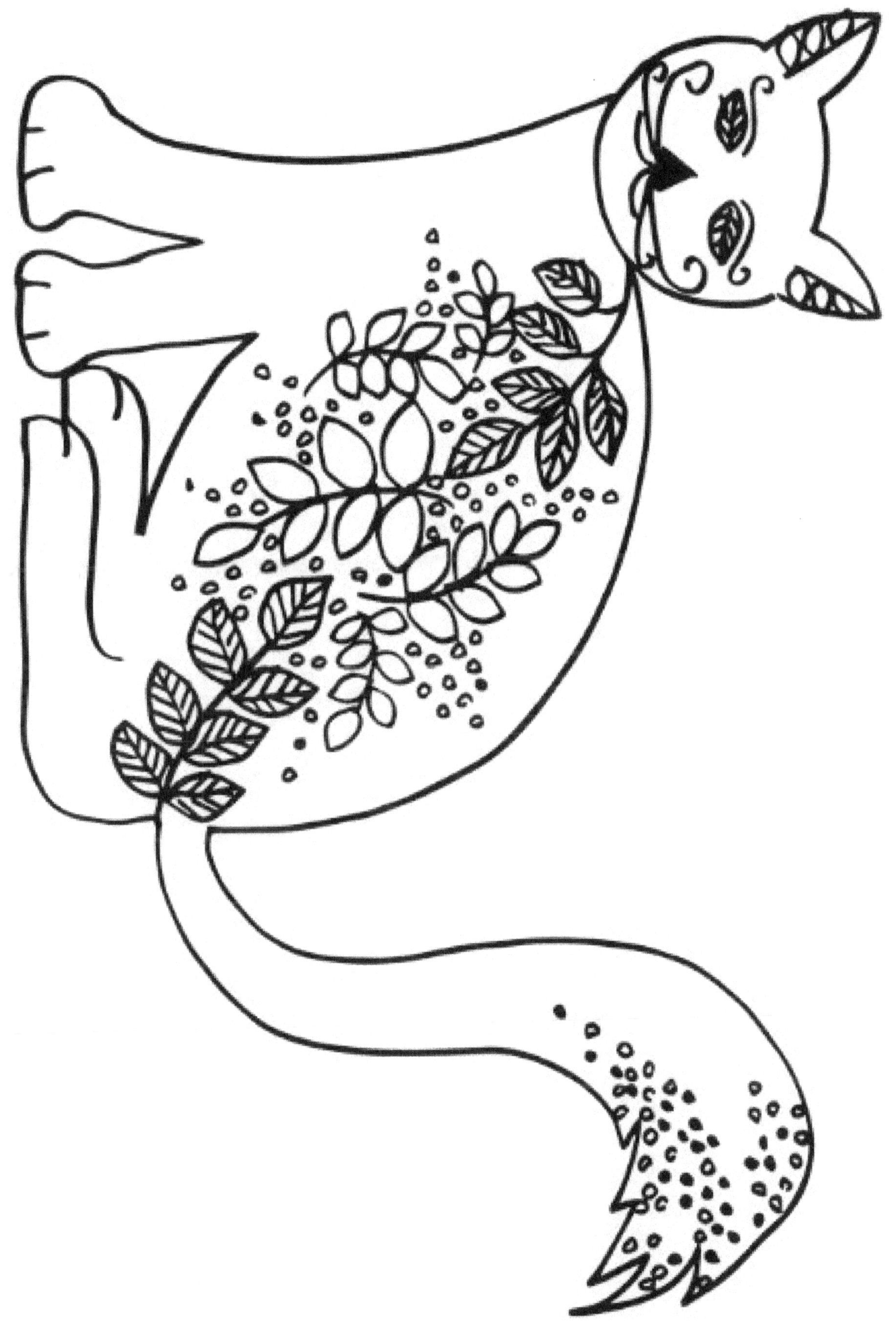

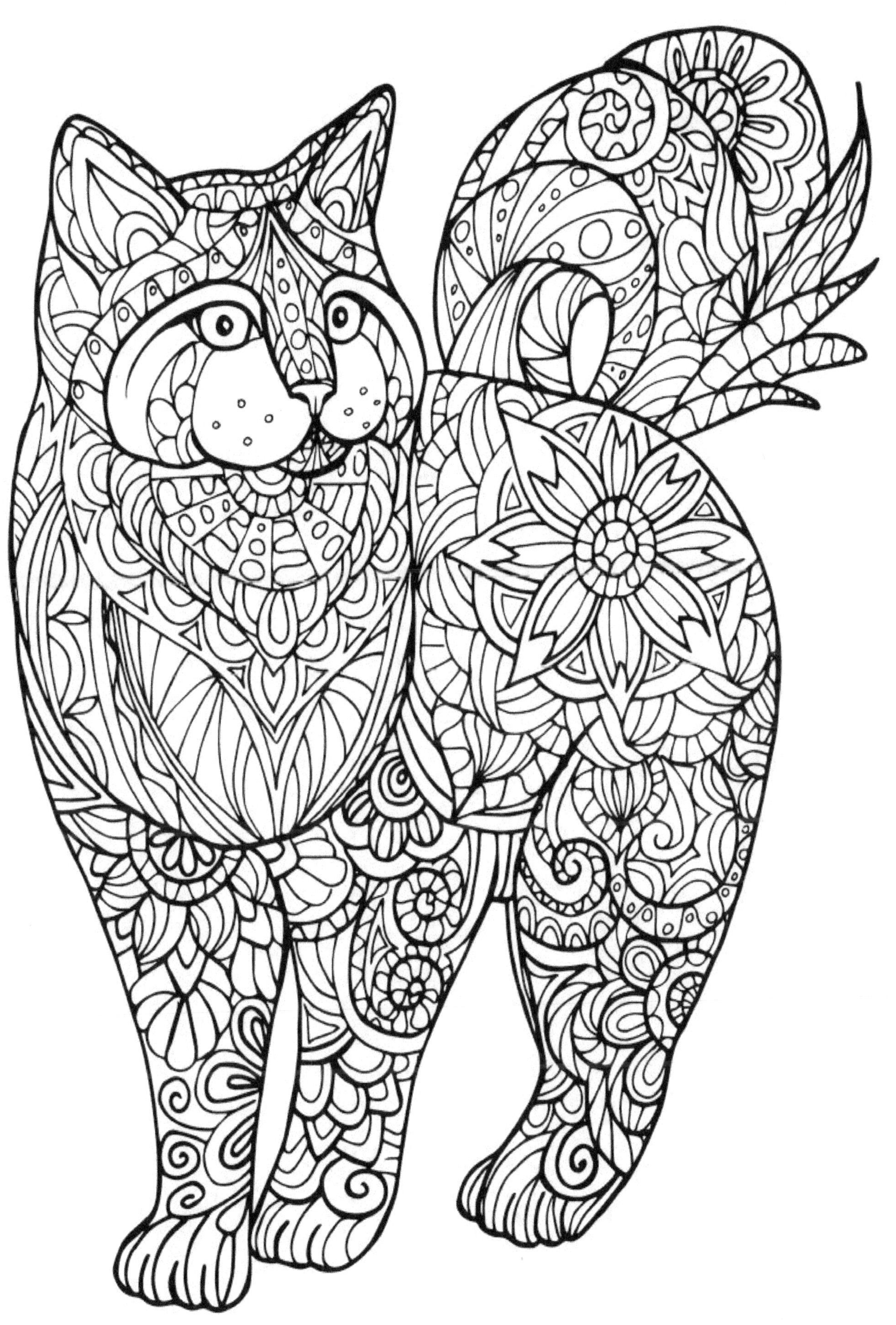

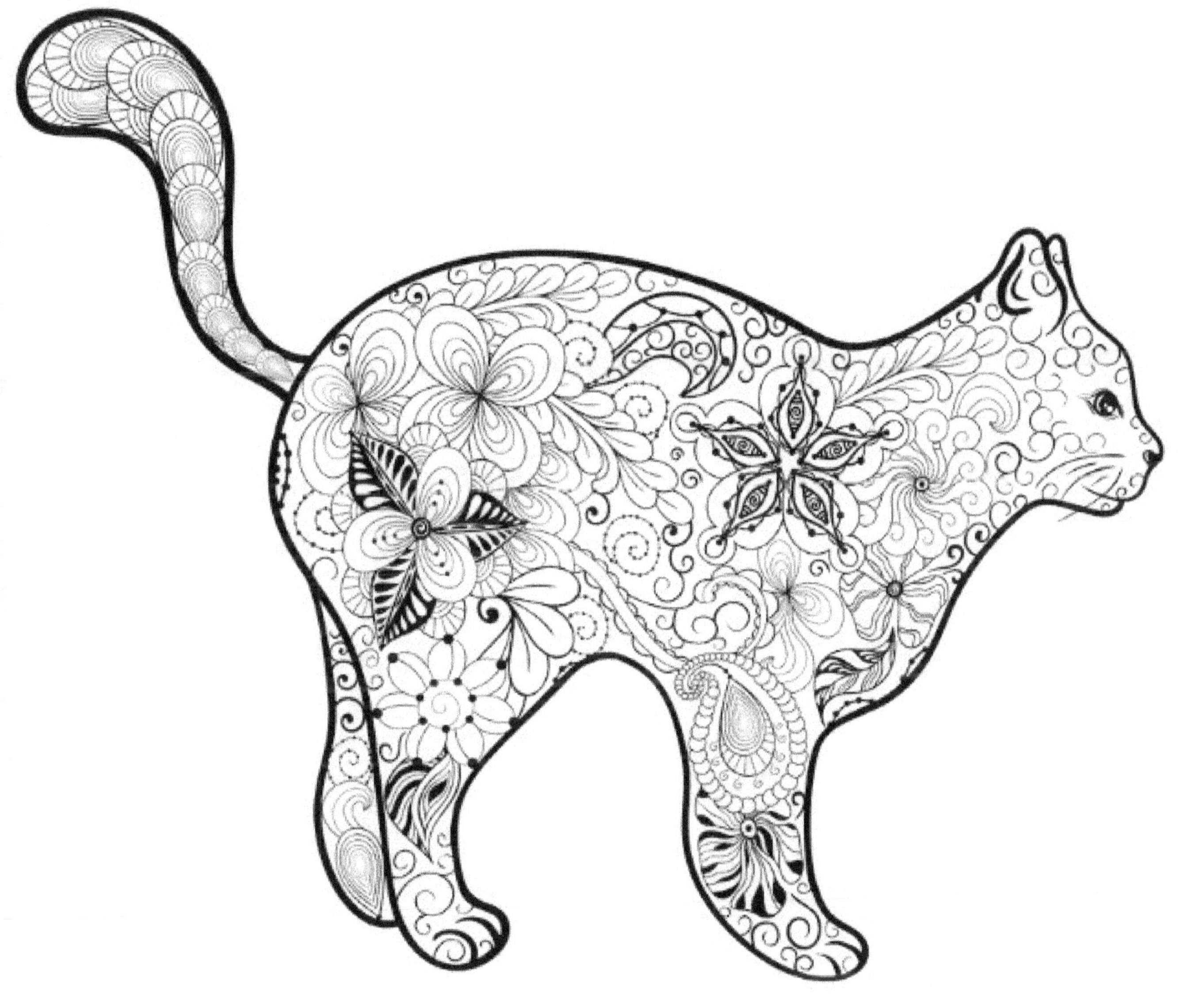

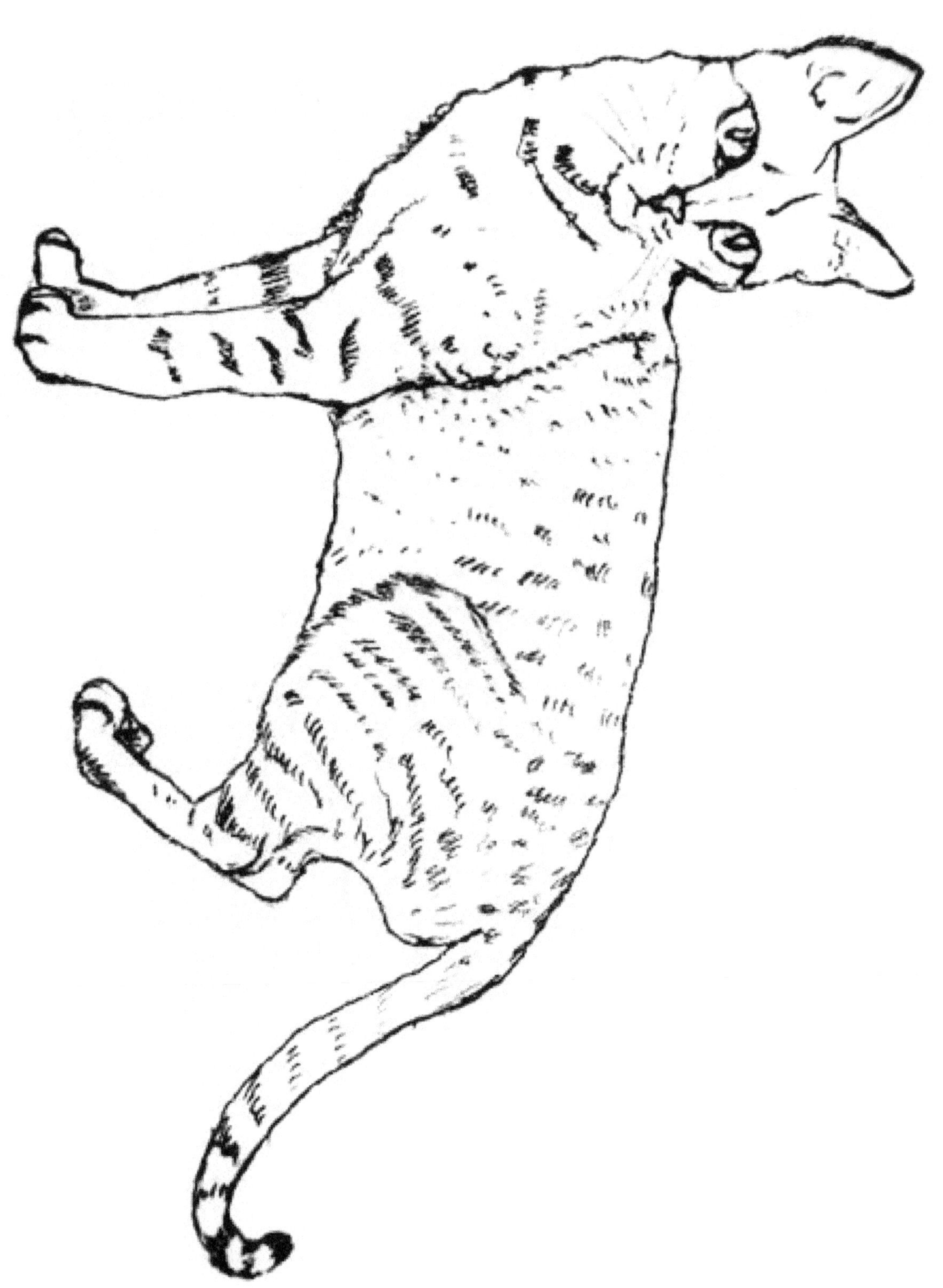

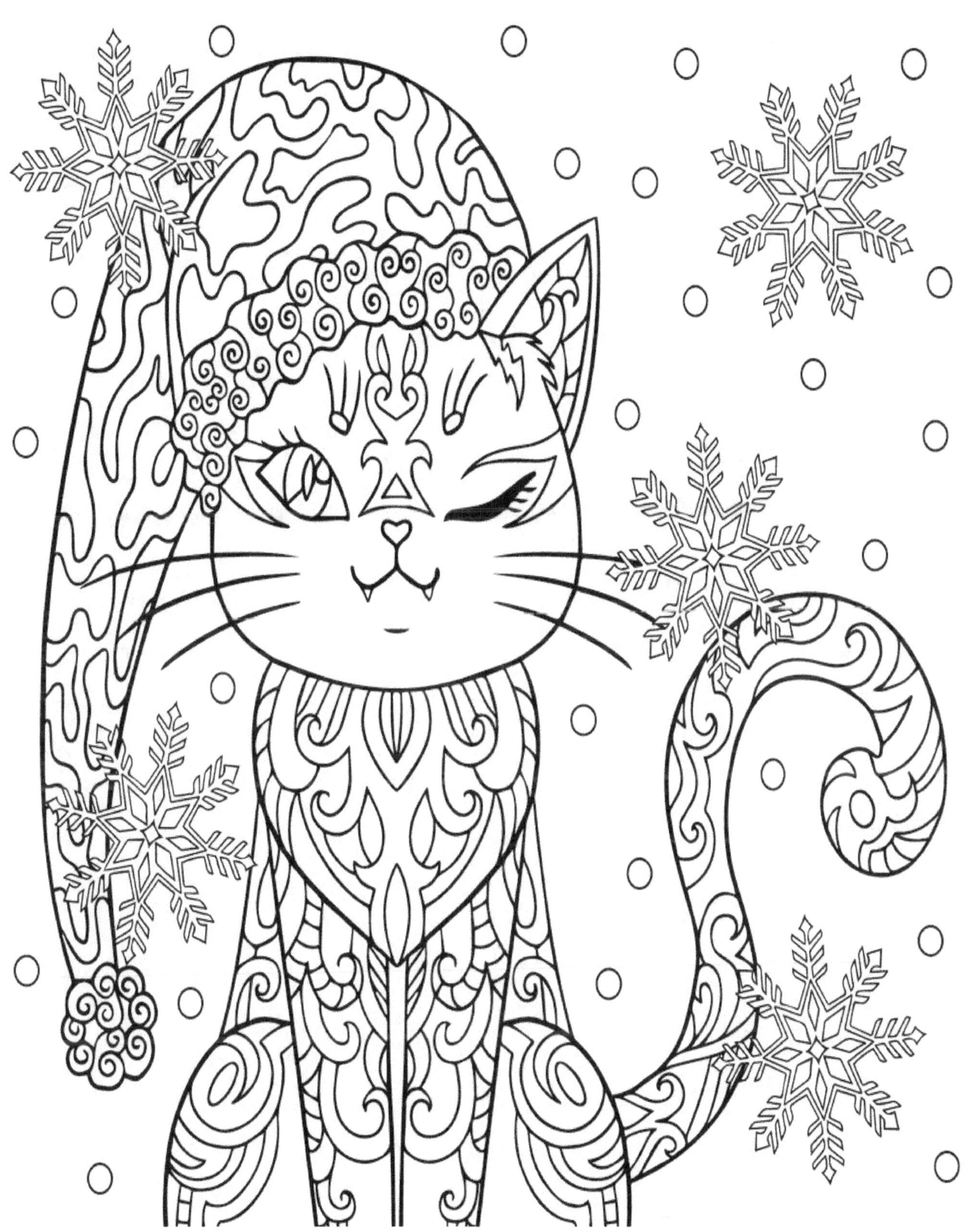

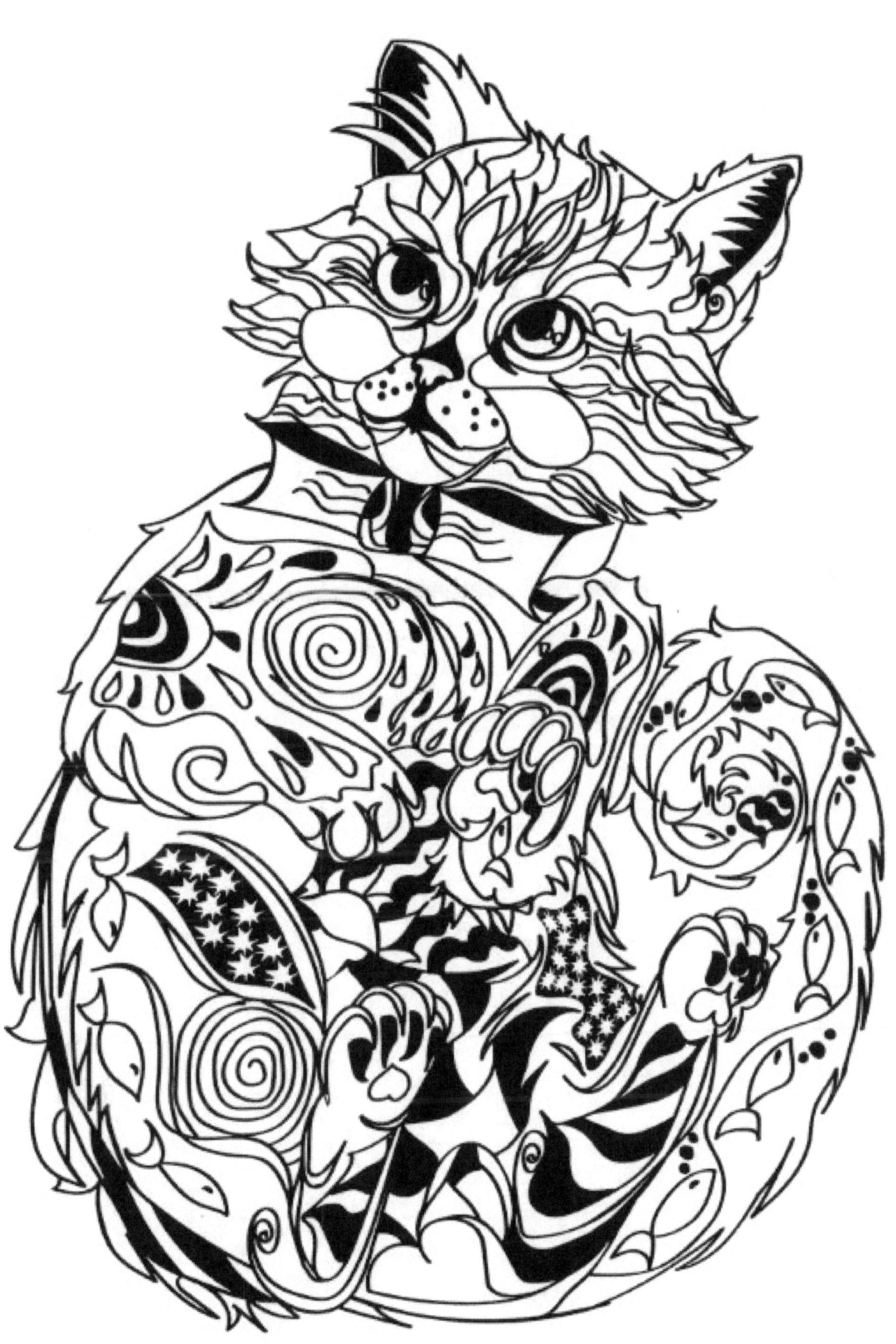

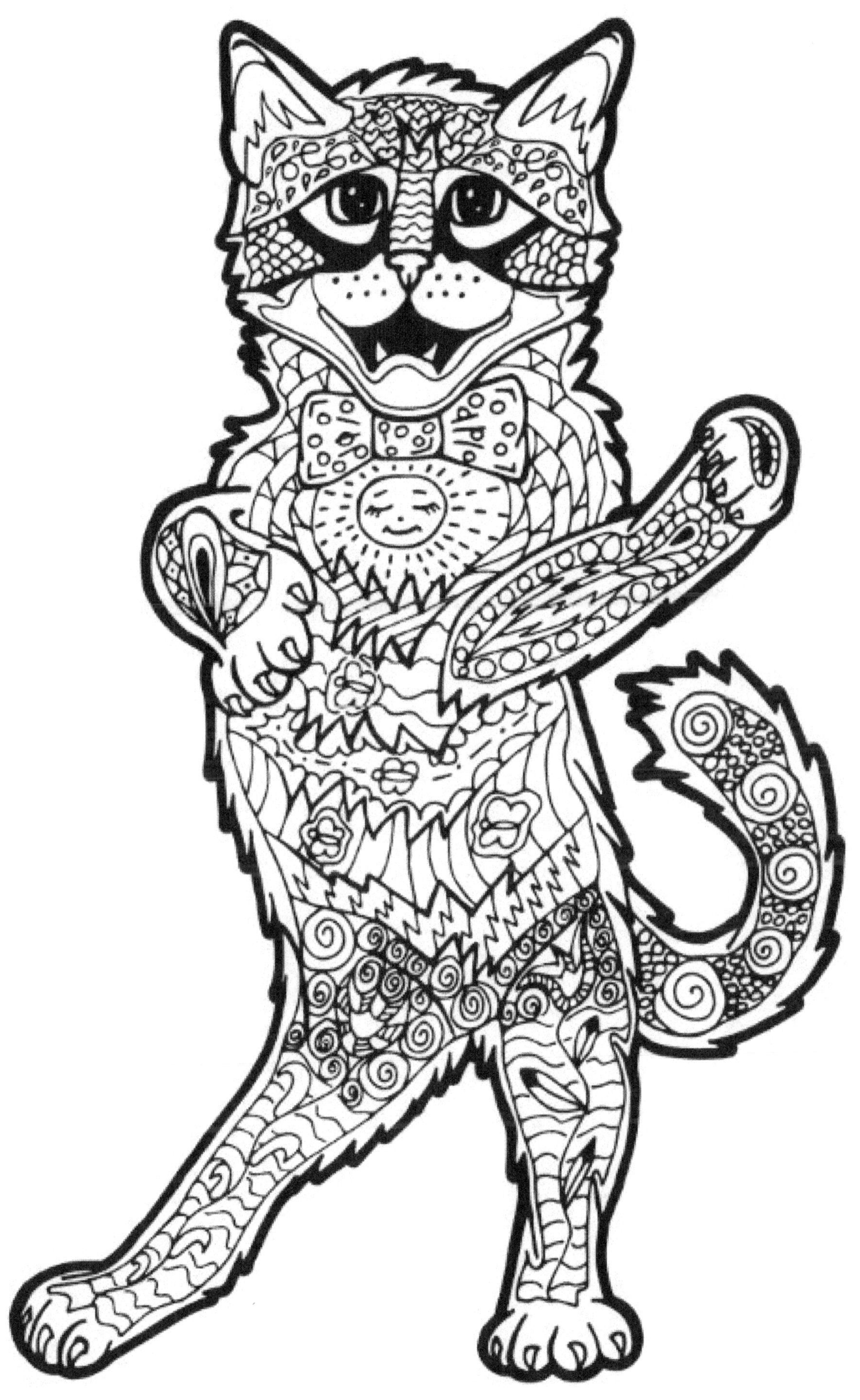

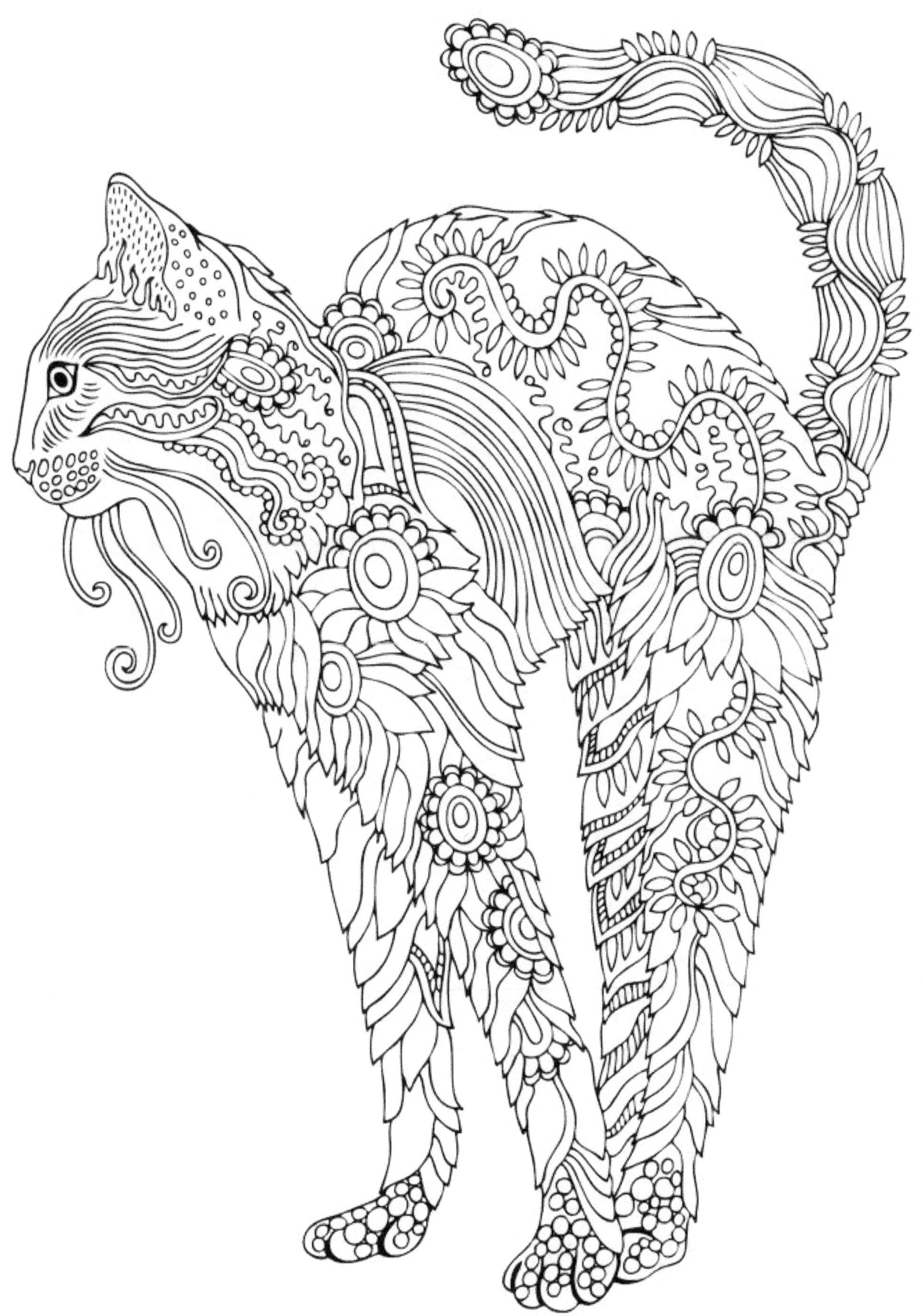

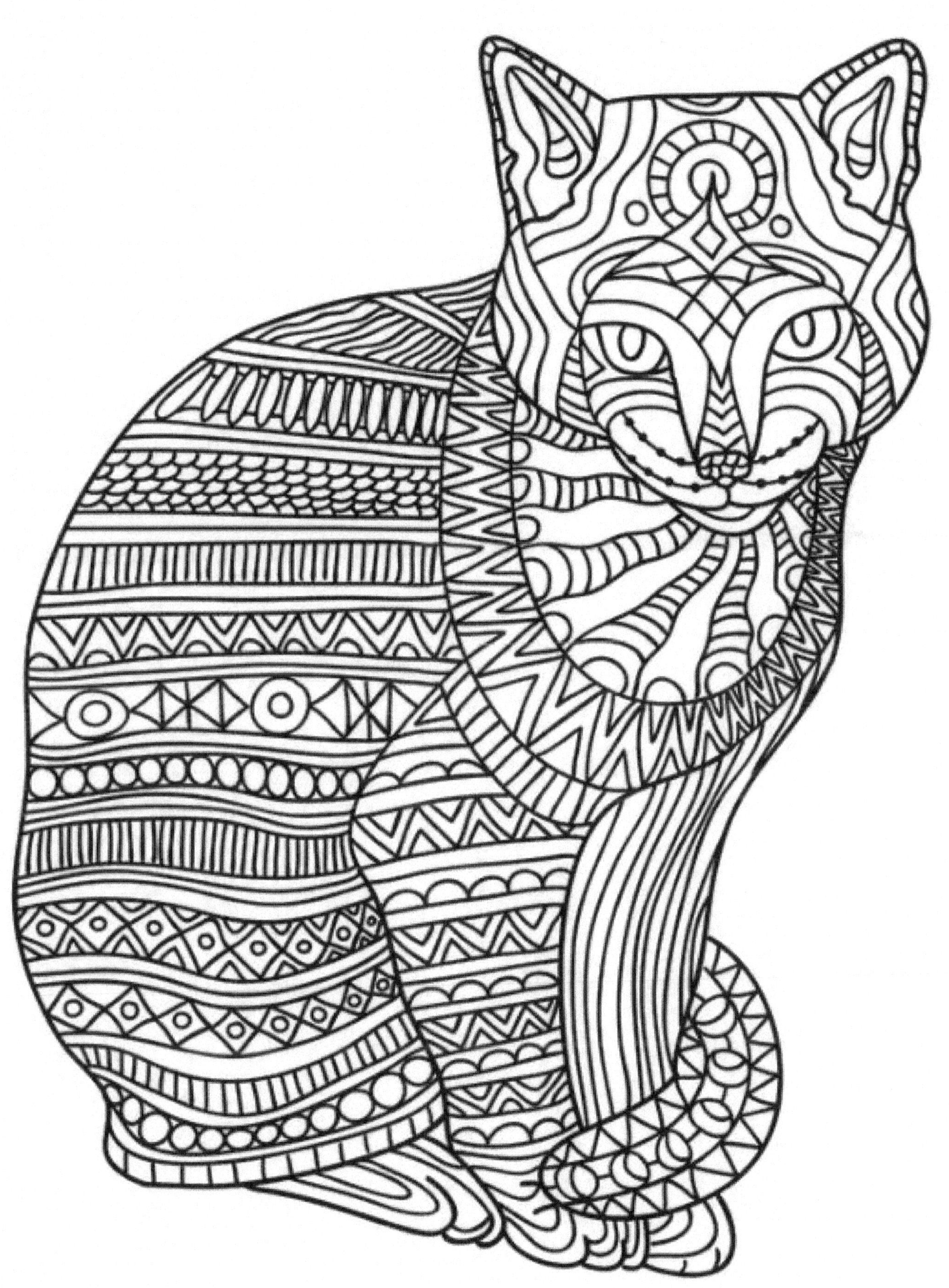

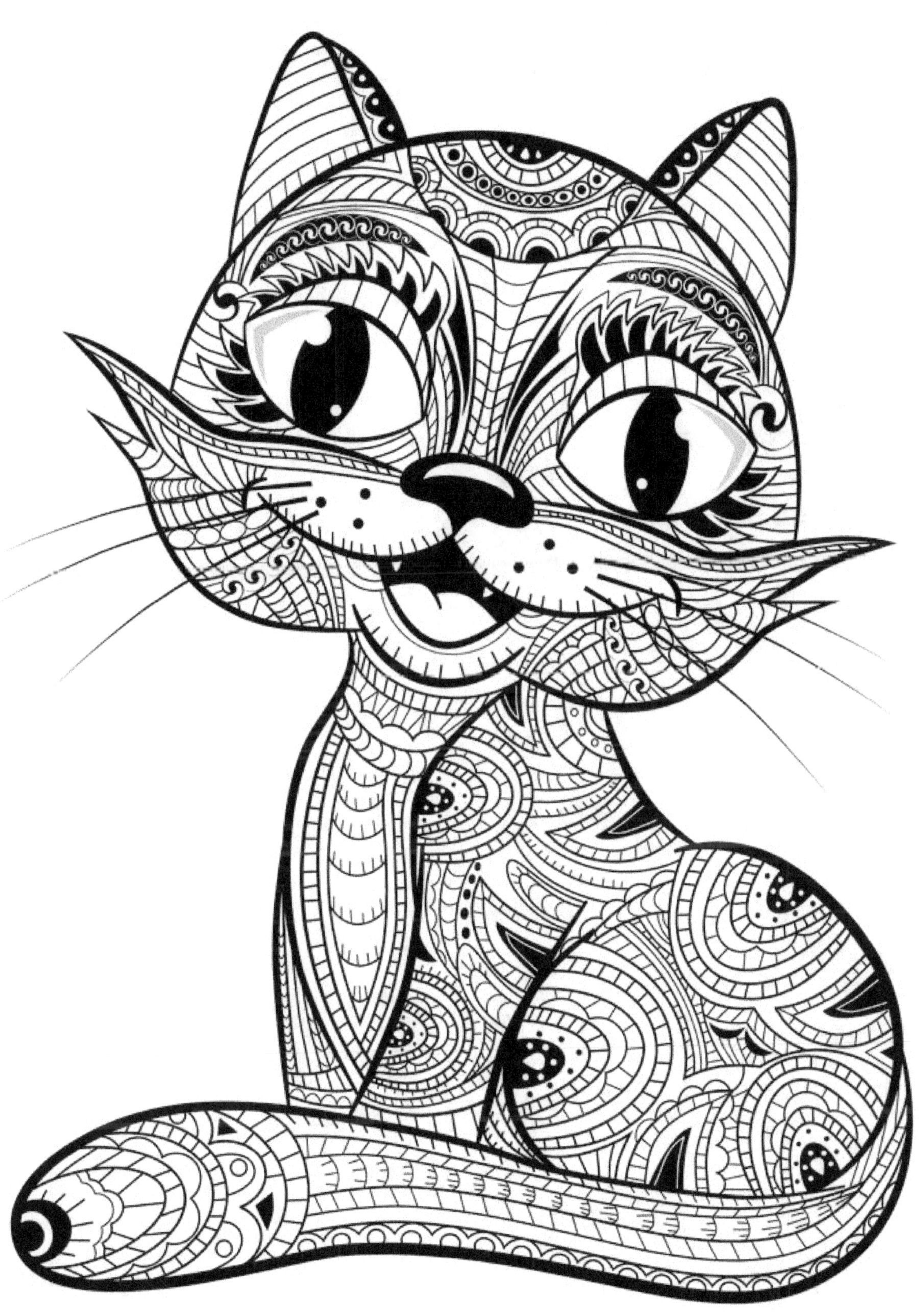

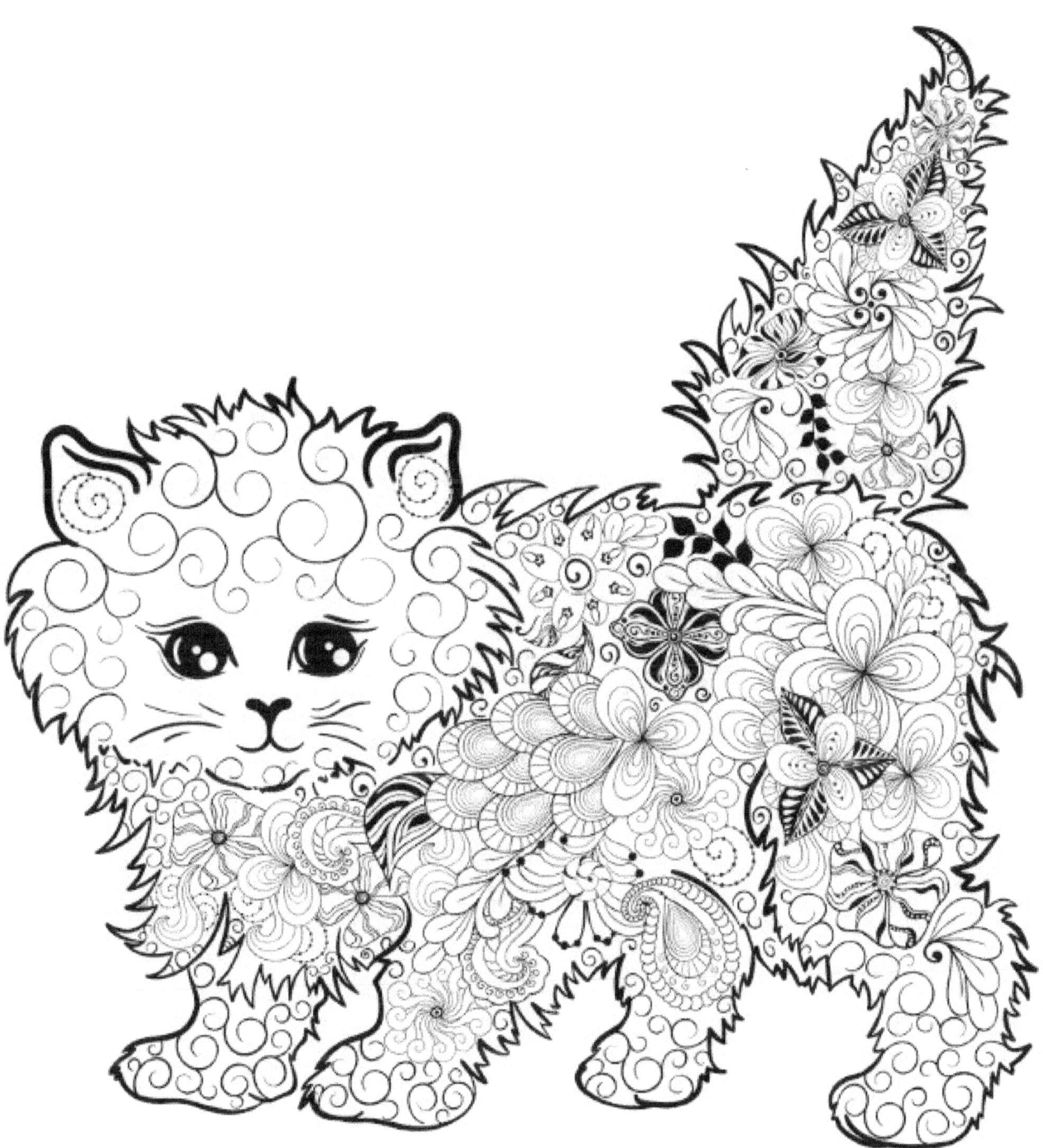

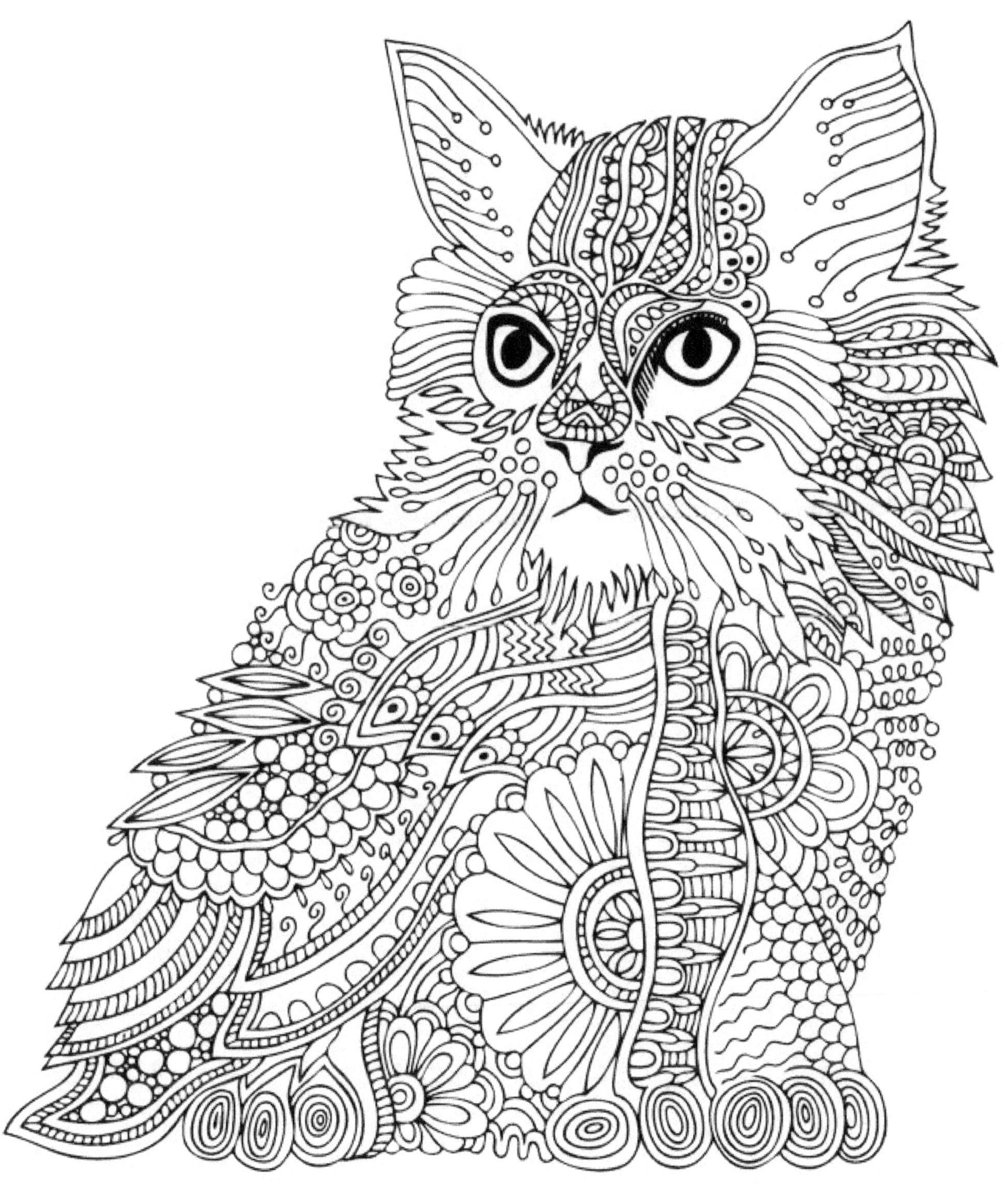

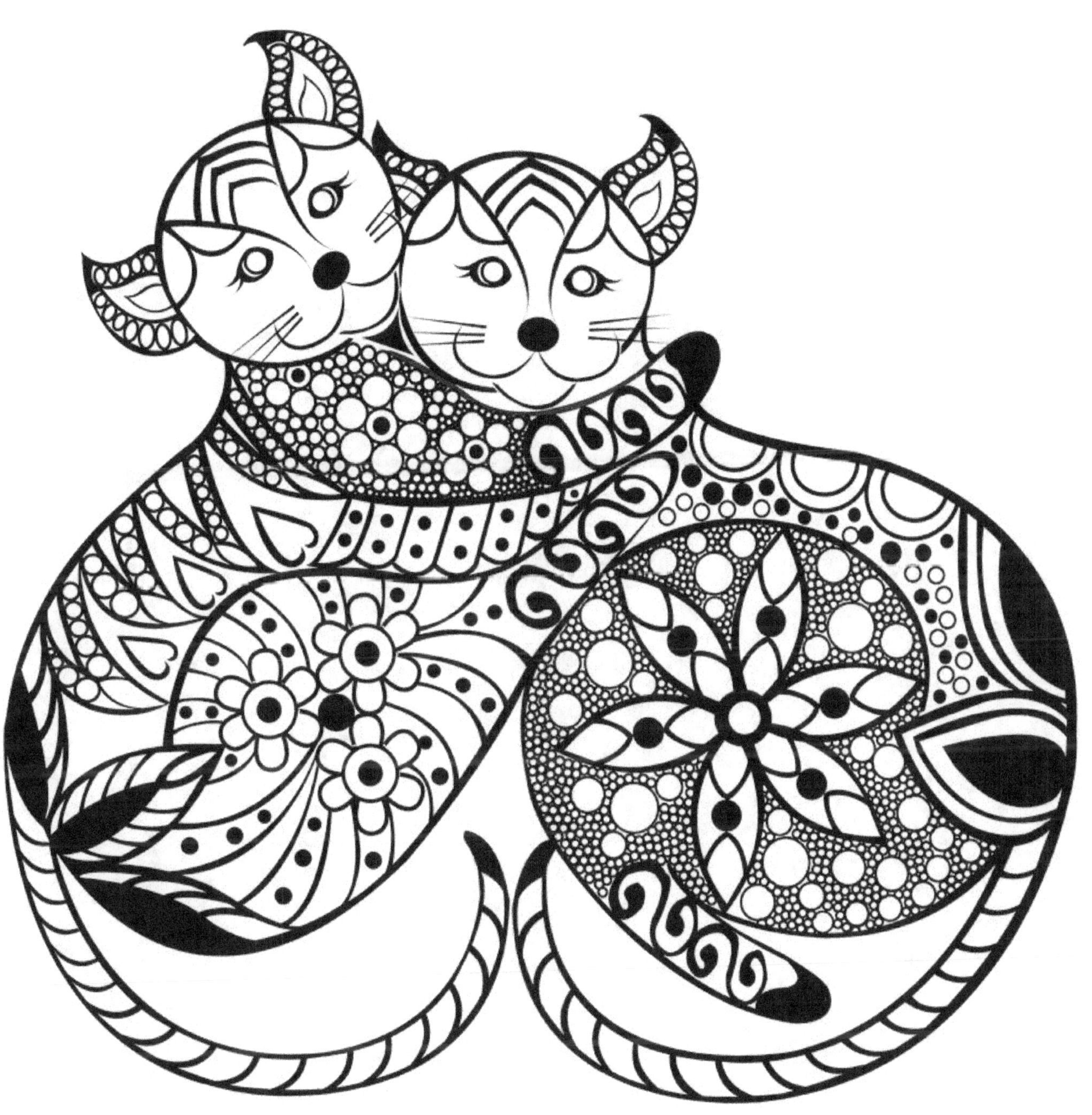

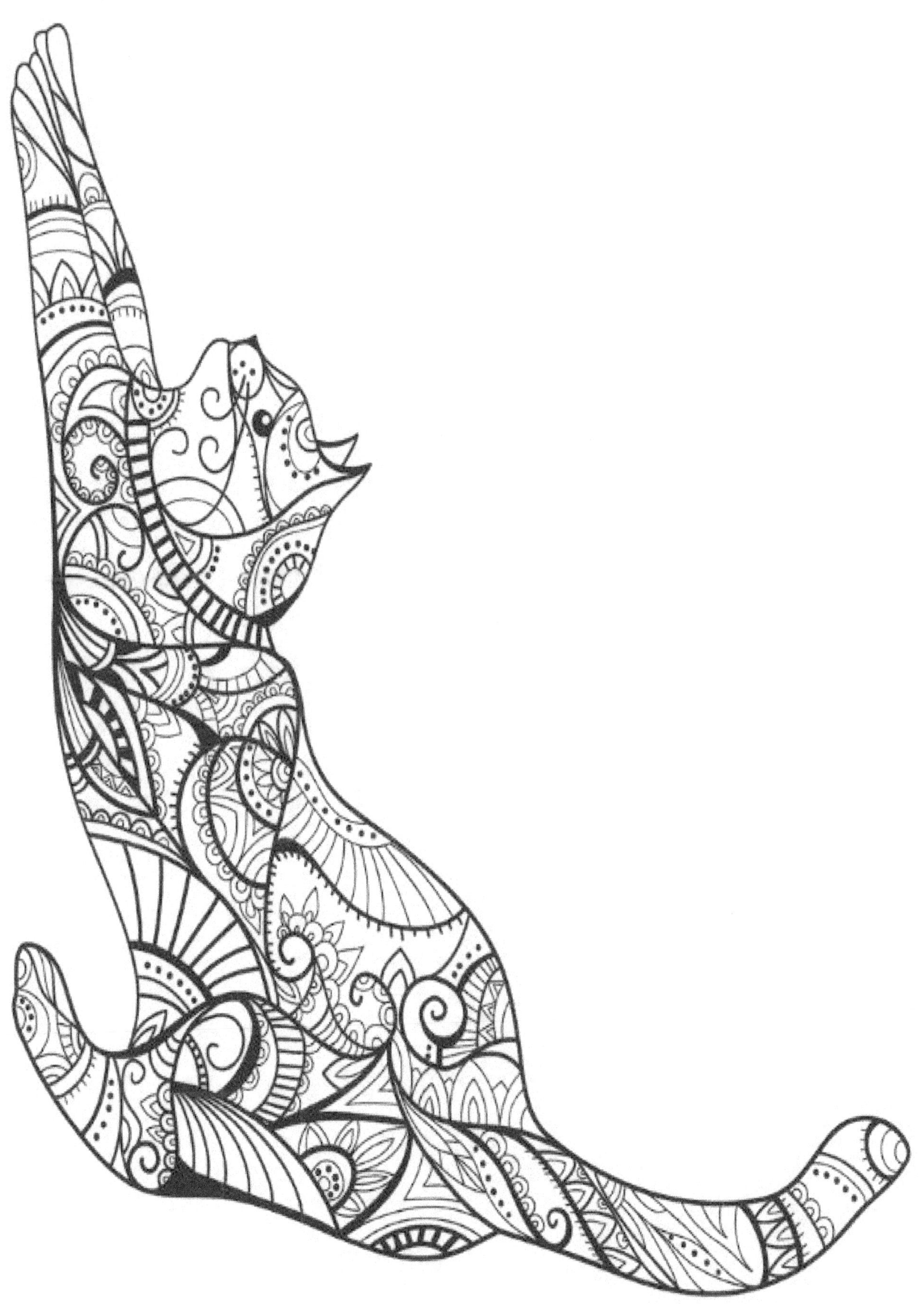

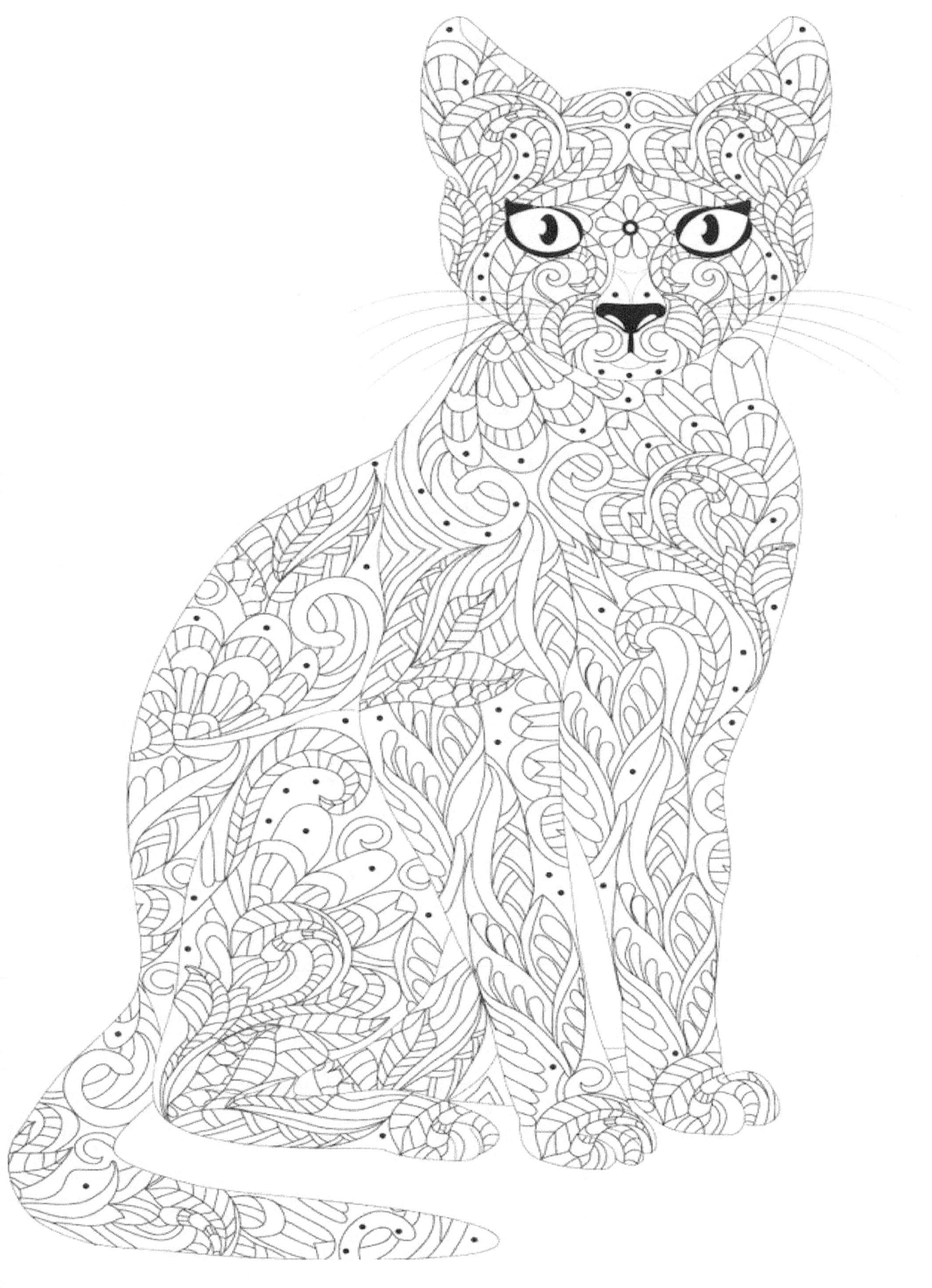

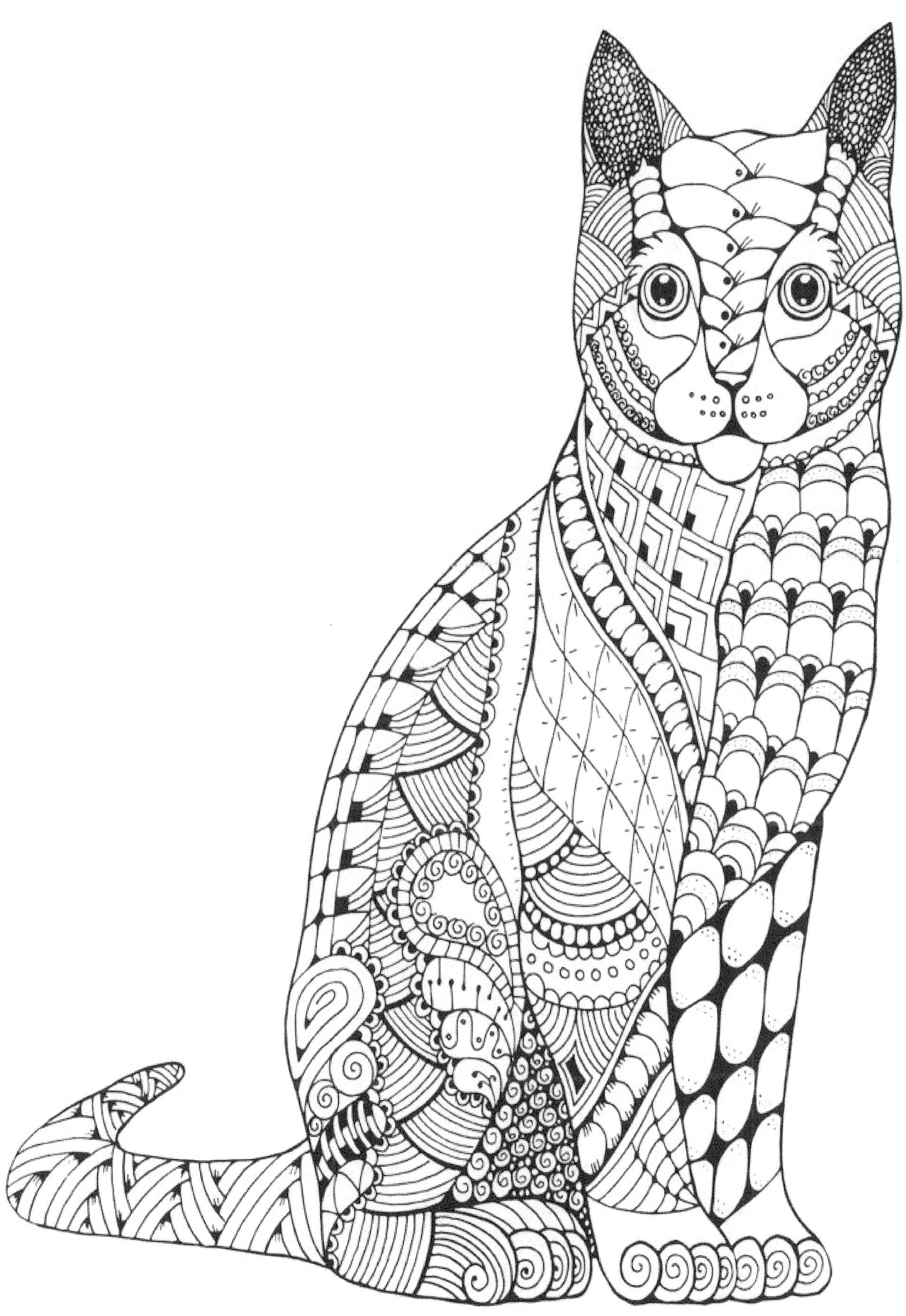

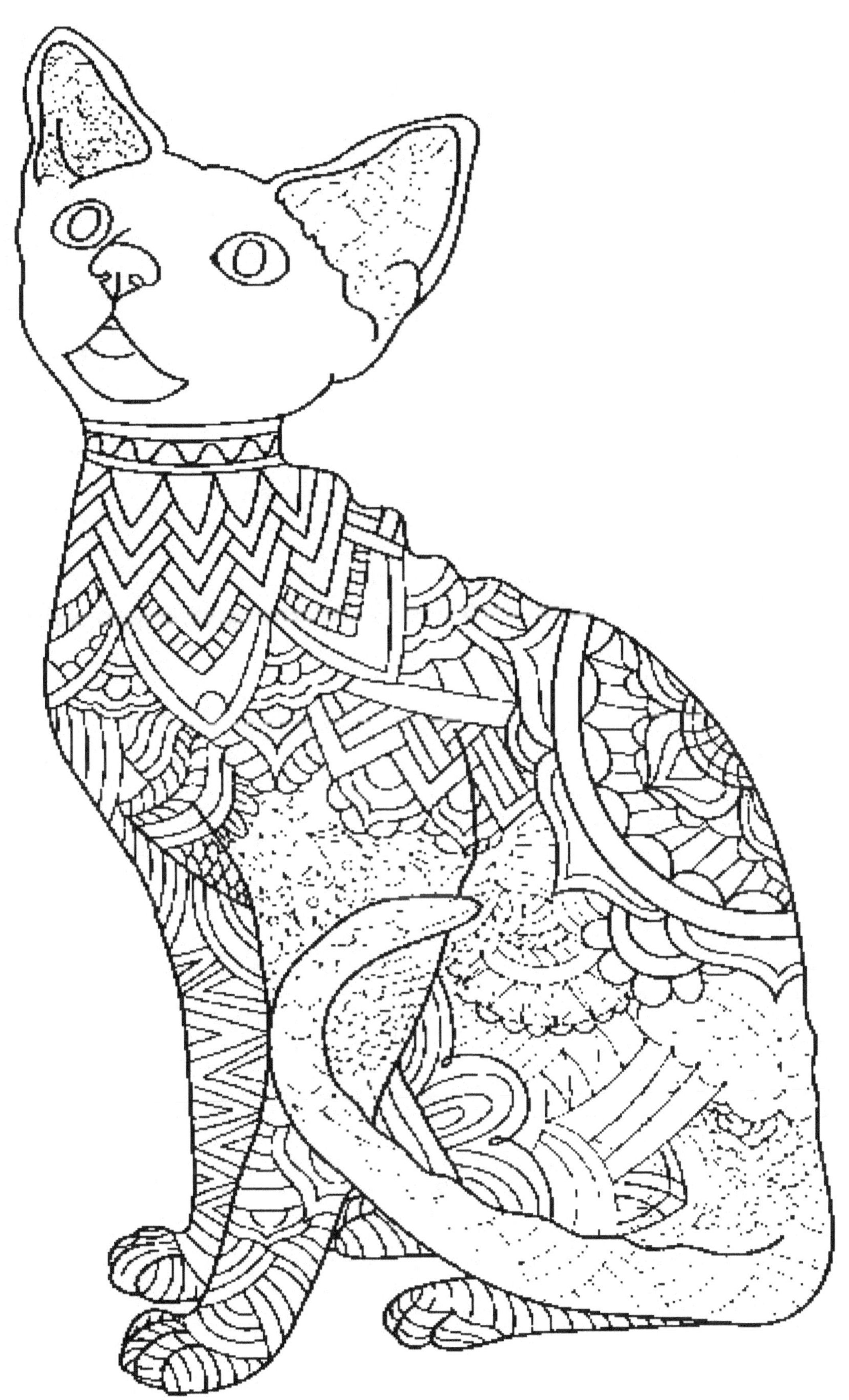

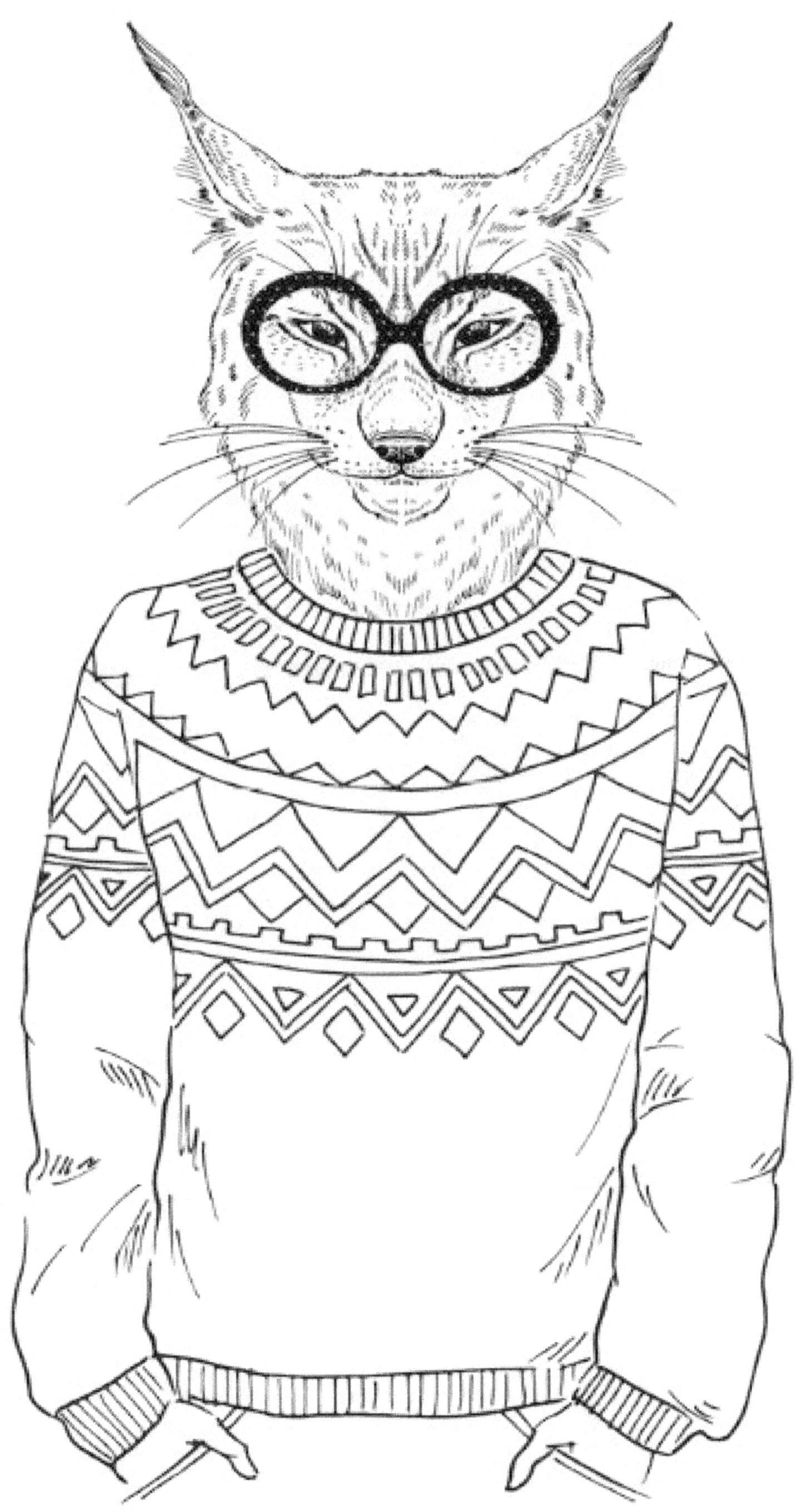

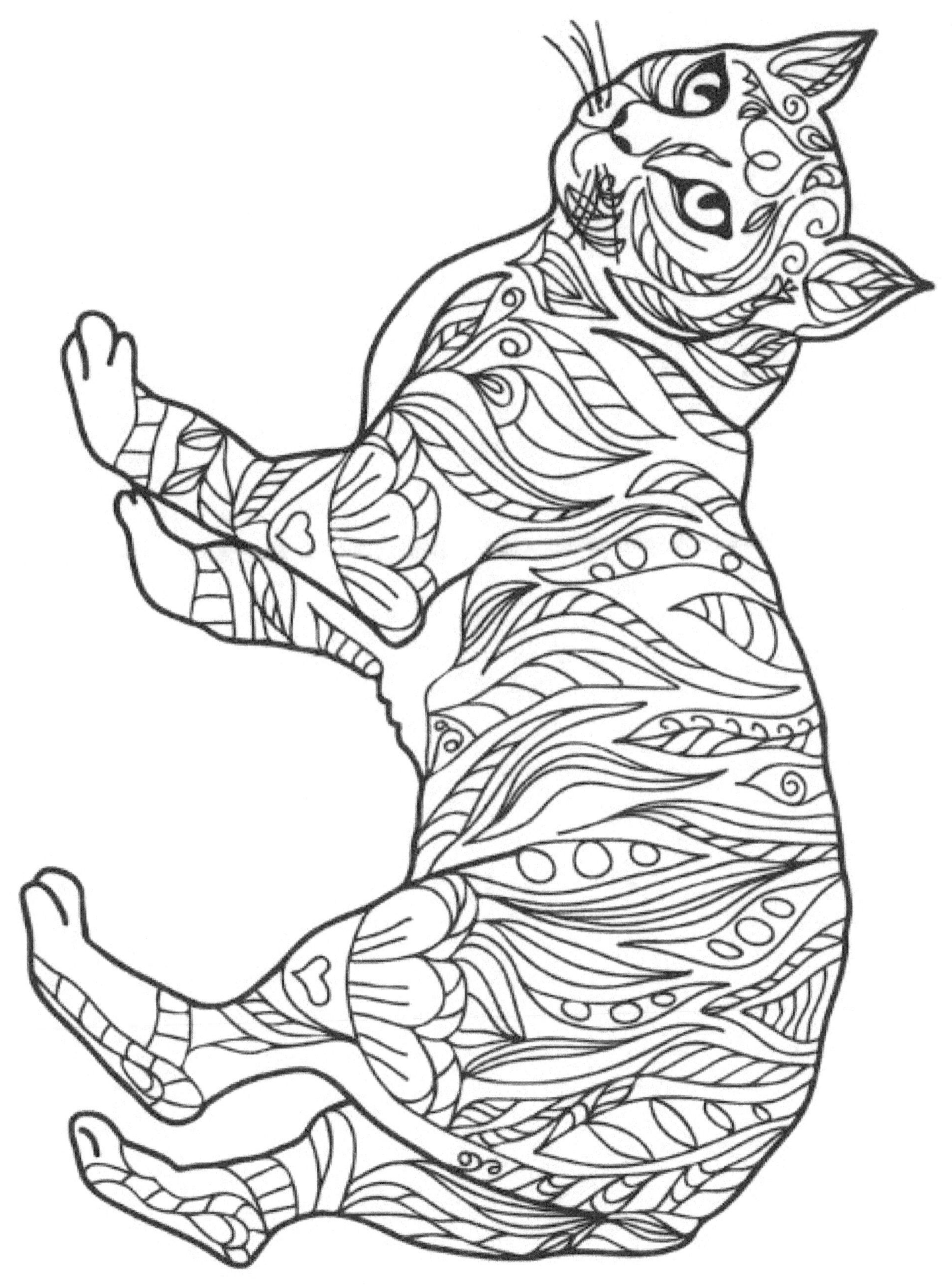

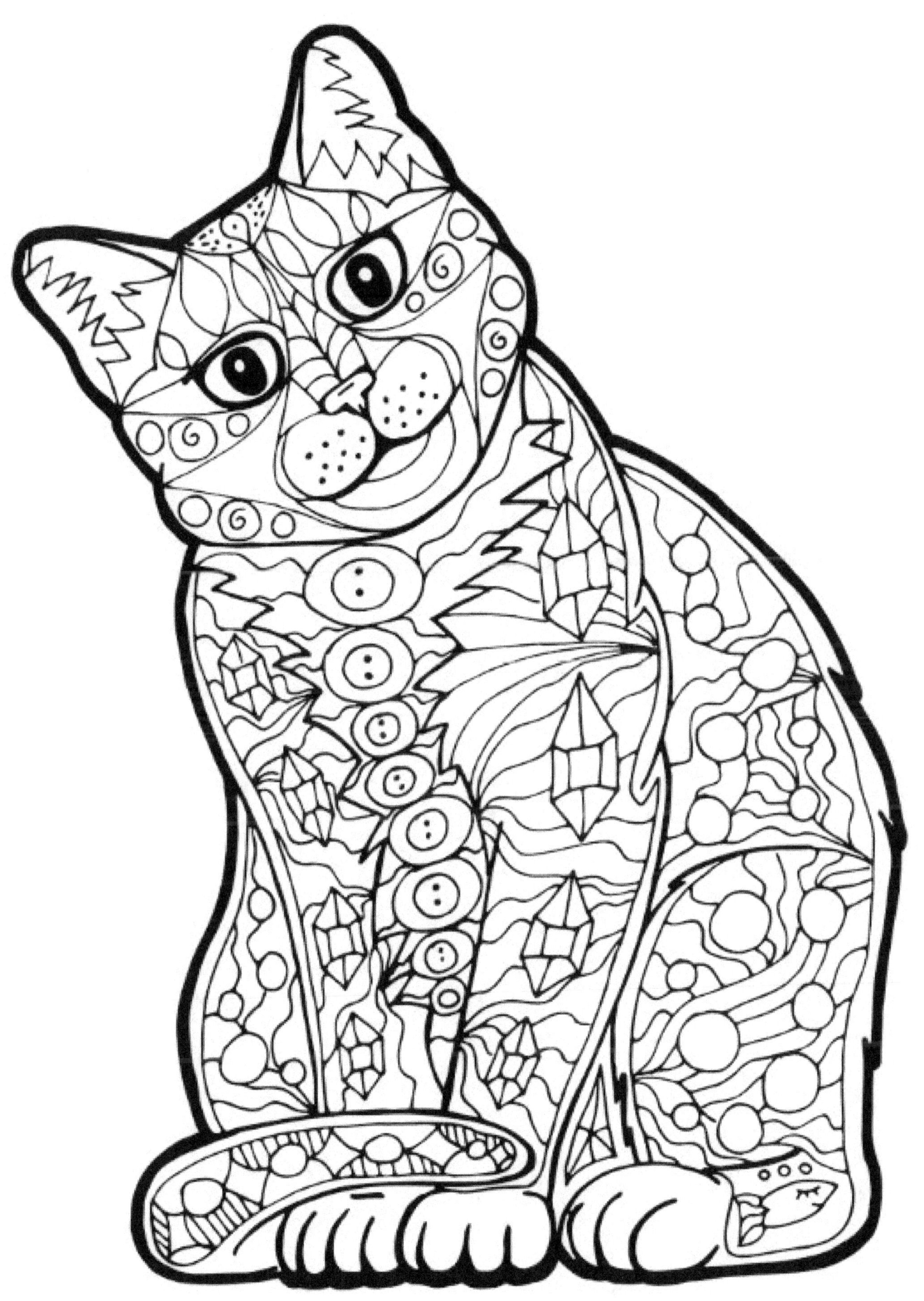

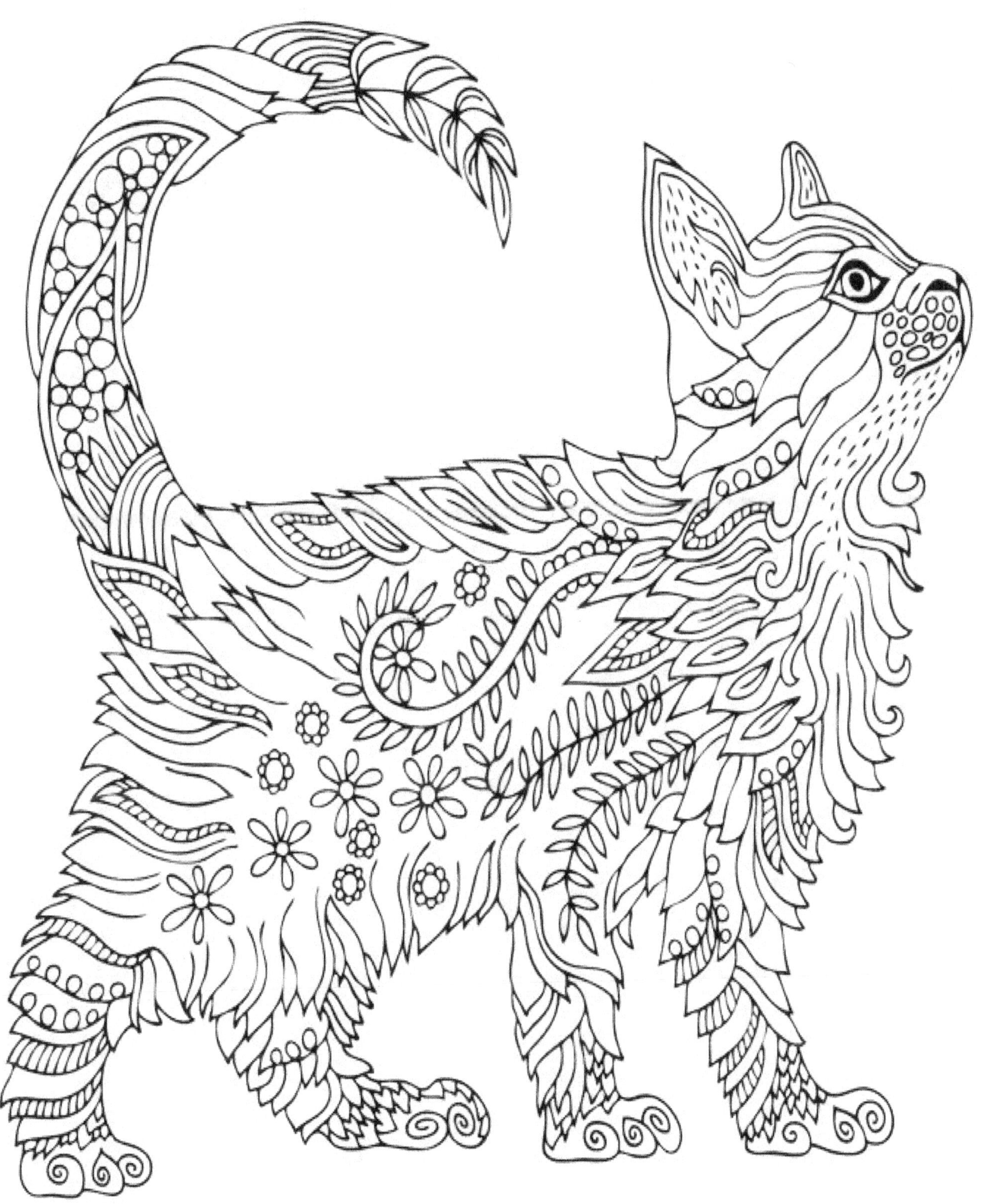

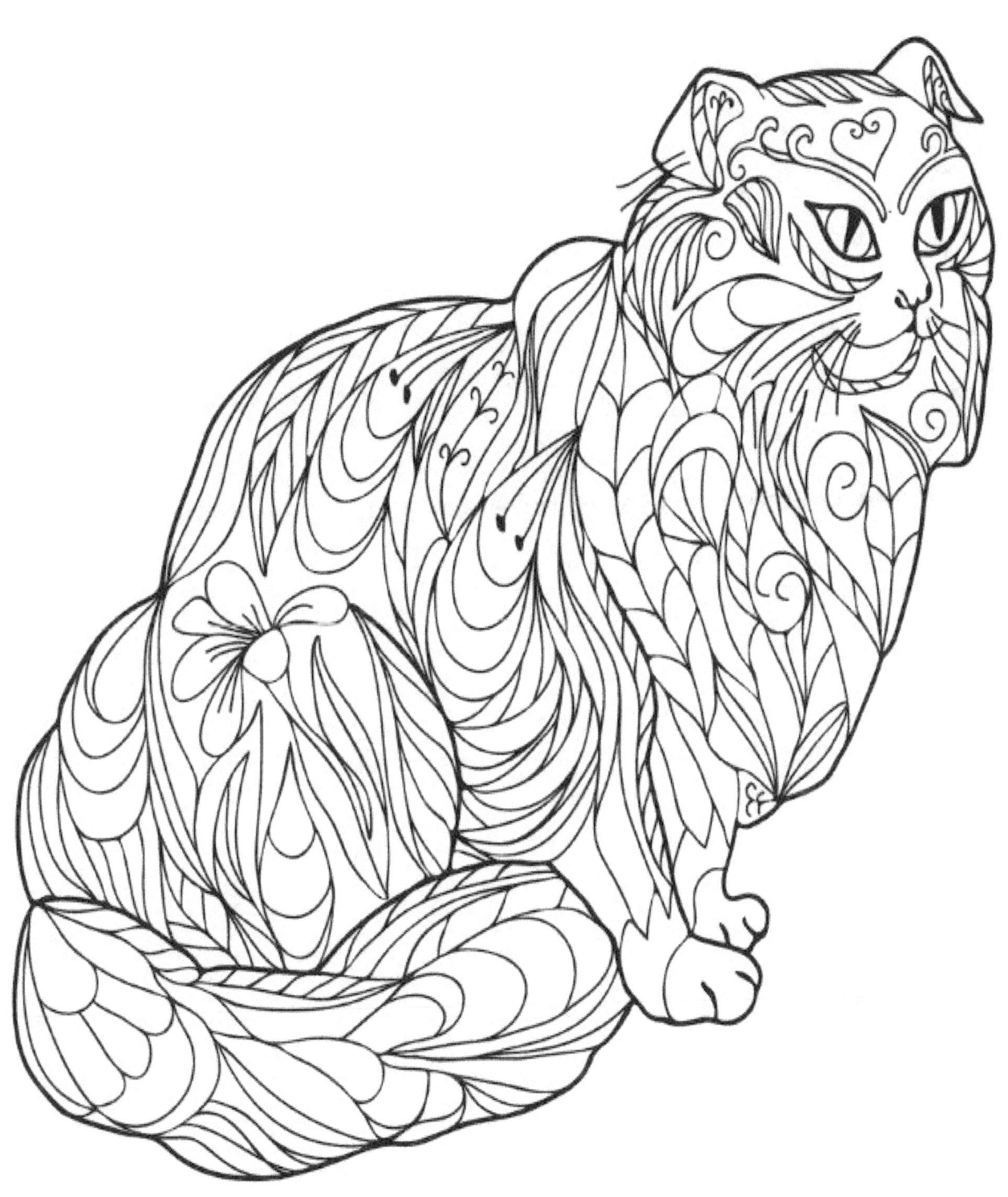

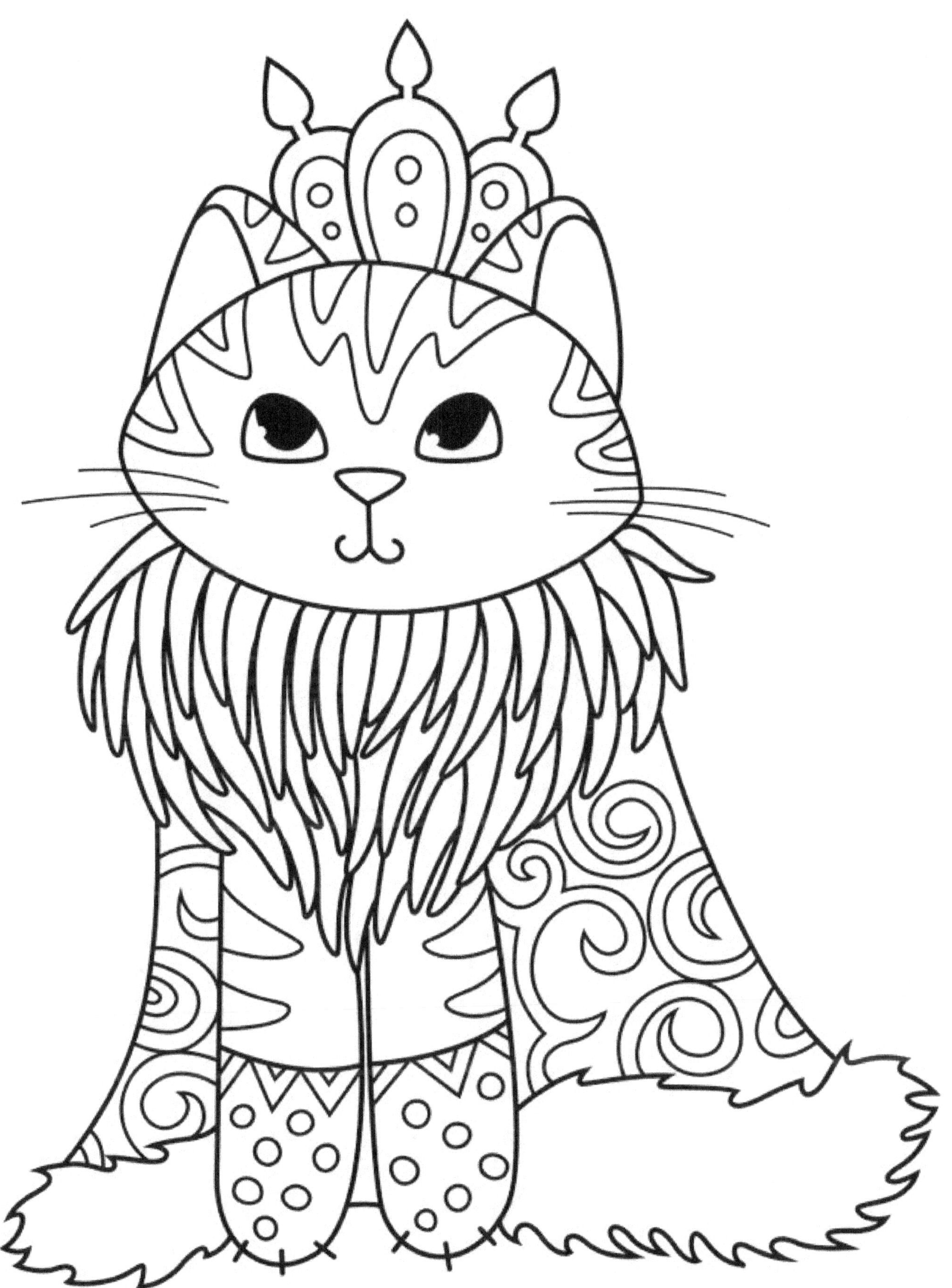

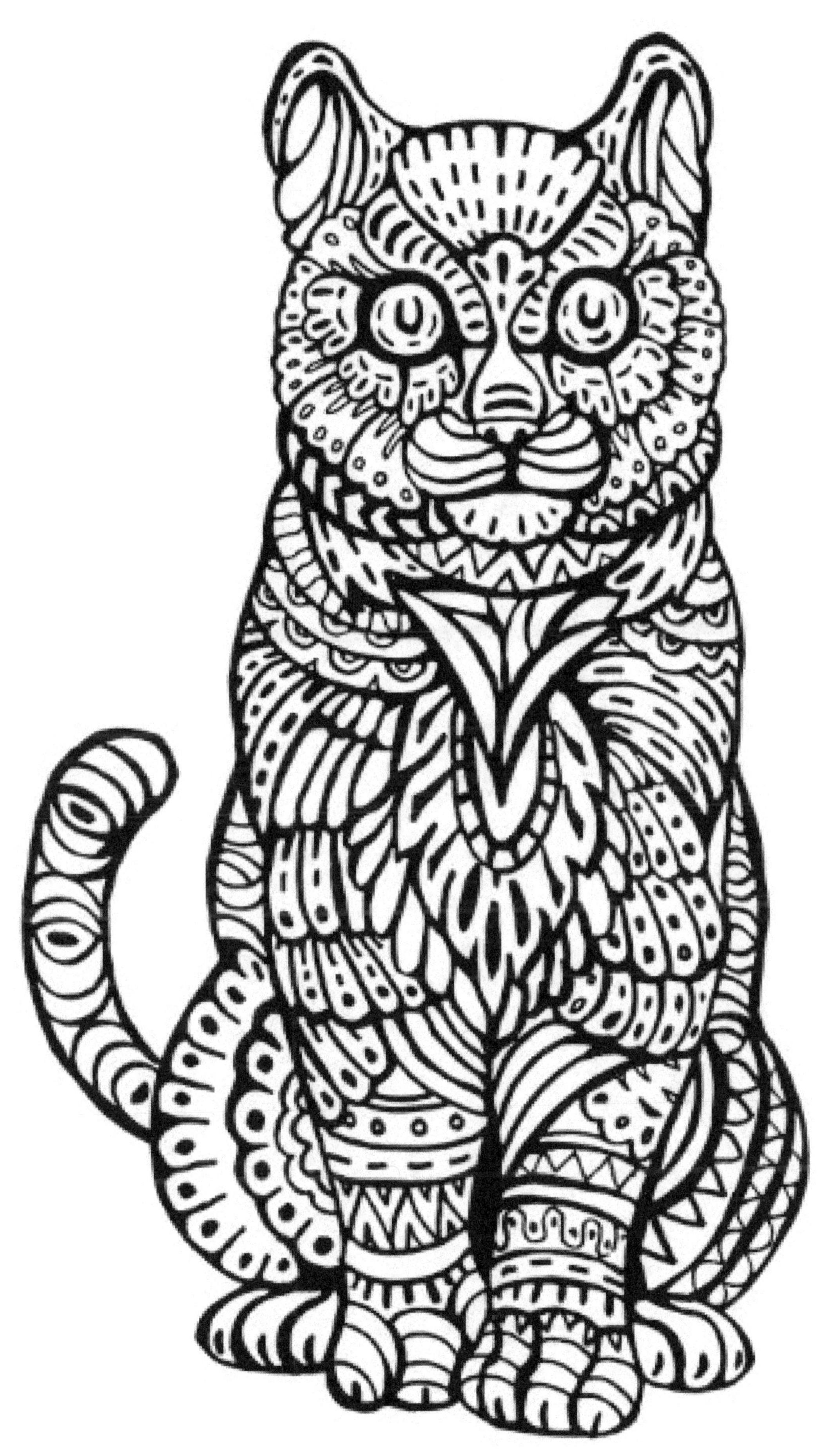

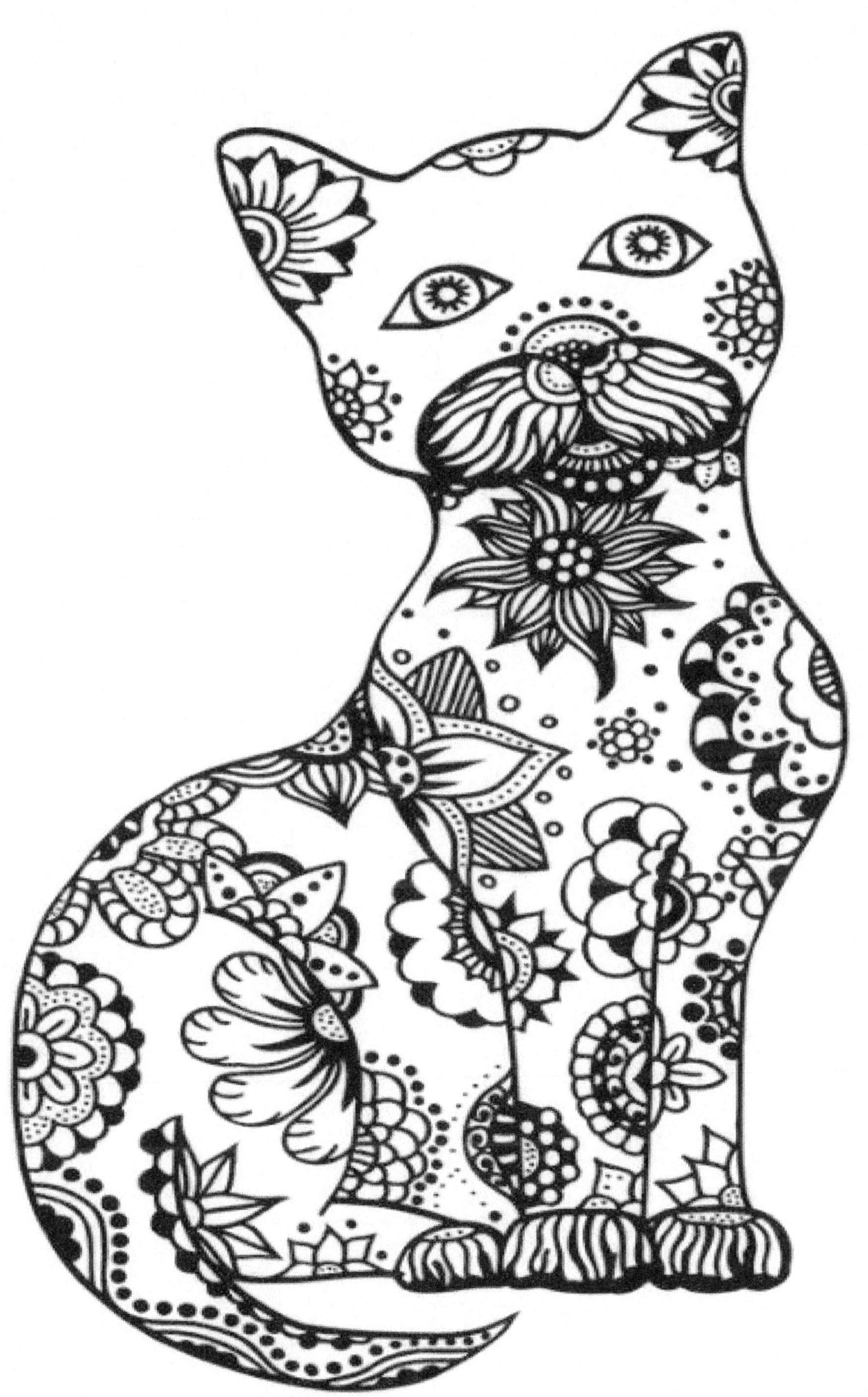

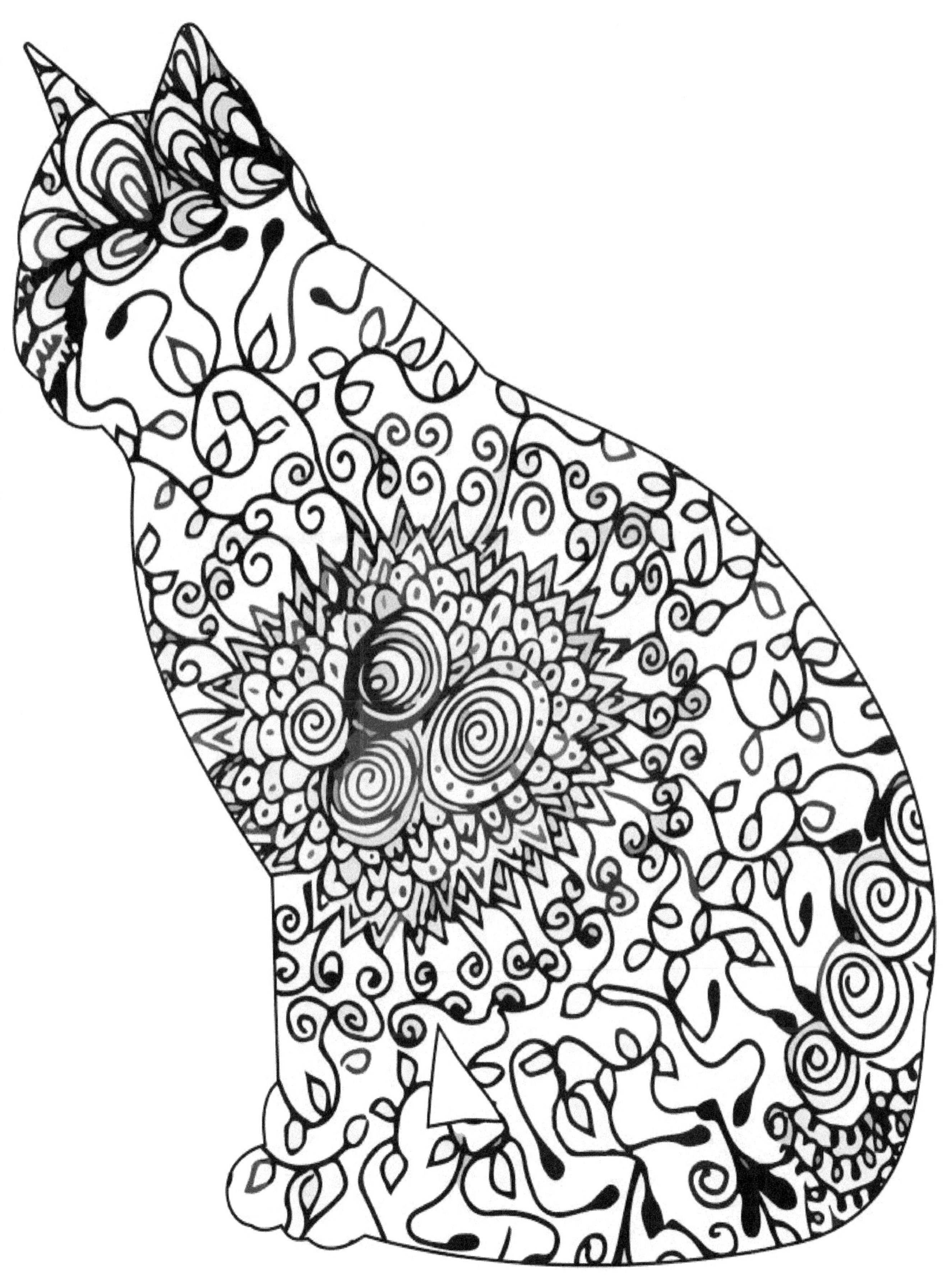